MW01041574

Social Studies

Social Studies

The Best of *The Globe and Mail*'s Daily Miscellany of Information

Michael Kesterton

with cartoons by Brian Gable

M&S

Canadian Cataloguing in Publication Data
Kesterton, Michael, 1946–
    Social studies

ISBN 0-7710-4451-8

1. Curiosities and wonders. I. Title.

AG243.K46 1996   031.02   C95-933198-0

The publisher acknowledges the support of the Canada Council and the Ontario Arts Council for their publishing program.

Typesetting by M&S, Toronto
Printed and bound in Canada on acid-free paper

McClelland & Stewart Inc.
The Canadian Publishers
481 University Avenue
Toronto, Ontario
M5G 2E9

1 2 3 4 5   00 99 98 97 96

January

Blame Napoleon?

On January 1, 1799, income tax was introduced in Britain –
to help fight Napoleon – by Prime Minister William Pitt the
Younger. Income tax is still around, in many countries. Paying
up has inspired much ingenuity. Some Canadian cases:

• 1946. Russell Rogers Smith of Saskatoon refused to file his
1943 federal return, claiming that Canada doesn't legally exist.
The judge, pointing to the British North America Act, fined
him $25.

• 1948. William Bremner of Toronto said he failed to file
returns for 1942-44 because he thought Ottawa's letters were
for William Bremner, his cousin. Fined $75 and costs.

• 1949. Russell Rogers Smith – now of Verdun, Quebec – was
still claiming Canada didn't exist. Fined $250.

• 1950. Robert Evans of Toronto said he filed incomplete

returns for 1942-44, and no returns for 1945-48, because his job at the post office kept him so busy he didn't have time for the paperwork. Fined $120.

• 1957. Arthur Fountain of Orillia said he didn't file a tax return because he didn't have the education to do so. The judge, citing his earlier returns, fined him $25.

• 1962. Wilfrid Lalonde of Ottawa said the mice in his attic chewed up $6,000 worth of his bond coupons, so he didn't report the assets. Fined $2,150. (Source: *Globe* files.)

In times to come ...

January 4, 1643, was the birthday of Isaac (Gravity) Newton, which calls to mind the Andromeda Galaxy, the most distant object a person can see with the naked eye. That smudge of light is only 2.2 million light years away and coming our way. The Hubble telescope has found evidence that Andromeda is a "cannibal," not yet finished attracting and devouring a galaxy it swallowed a billion years ago. In 11 billion years, it will collide with our Milky Way and suck it into its maw. Although the Earth and our sun will then be long gone, our descendants may still exist. From their point of view, says Hubble researcher Dr. Ray Villard, "their night skies will fill up with beautiful new structures of gas and dust."

The neckties that bind

Depending on whom you ask, when a man wraps a tie around his neck he is flaunting a phallic symbol or just showing off a decoration that has been used for centuries to mark a man as something special:

• The earliest known ties come from the tomb of China's first emperor, says Sarah Gibbings in her book *The Tie: Trends and Traditions*. Shih Huang Ti was buried with a terracotta army of 7,500 soldiers, each wearing a carefully wrapped silk neckcloth.

• The Romans thought that neckcloths were for the sickly or the effeminate. But crack troops of the victorious emperor Trajan, presumably being neither, were portrayed wearing them in AD 113.

• Cravats appeared on soldiers in the 17th century in France.

• The men in the family of Louis XIV wore long lace cravats that would have cost more than the average annual wage of the day. When Charles II regained England's throne in 1660, he wore a cravat that cost 20 pounds and 12 shillings, at a time when a few pounds was considered a good year's wages. (In 1990, Tokyo's Ginza was selling a necktie for $450 U.S.)

• Beau Brummel, who dictated that a man's individuality in clothes was limited to his cravat, began the cult of the neck-cloth. In 1827, the first international bestseller was published. The book described how to arrange a cravat.

• Young sports and dandies competed to find ways to knot their cravats. The modern tie is called a "four-in-hand" after a way of tying the reins of a four-in-hand carriage. The style stays in place regardless of how active the wearer may be.

• The first ready-made tie was patented in 1864 and was immediately sneered at.

• The first women cyclists began wearing neckties and suits, perhaps to show they were out in the streets for decent exercise.

• After both world wars, the necktie surged in popularity as demobilized soldiers abandoned their dull uniforms. During a brief tie mania in 1946, an American man might own 3,000 ties and belong to tie-swapping clubs.

• Worldwide, even in tropical countries, the necktie is currently worn as a symbol of wealth and the fact the wearer doesn't perform manual labour.

See no elephant

A newspaper in Calcutta has offered these survival tips when encountering a wandering elephant: Never stand in its path and, whatever you do, avoid eye contact.

For children's ears?

On January 4, 1785, Jacob Grimm was born. "For many adults, reading through an unexpurgated edition of the (Brothers) Grimms' collection of tales can be an eye-opening experience," contends Maria Tatar in her book *The Hard Facts of the Grimms' Fairy Tales*. The stories' rough stuff included murder, mutilation, cannibalism, infanticide, and incest, she writes. Notes about nursery stories:
• Many fairy tales and nursery rhymes derive from unsavoury folk tales for preliterate grownups. In any event, children were once regarded as miniature adults, says author Charles Panati, and were not shielded from bawdy language, sexual shenanigans, drunkenness – or public floggings, hangings, and disembowelments.
• Our fairy tales have been sanitized from earlier versions. Some details expunged: Sleeping Beauty was raped while unconscious by a married man and produced twins that his wife tried to feed to him; Little Red Riding Hood performed a "striptease" for the Big Bad Wolf; in one version of *Cinderella* (the story has been traced back 1,000 years) the child breaks her first stepmother's neck; the wicked queen in *Snow White*

was forced to dance to death in red-hot shoes; Goldilocks was an angry, homeless old woman dropping in on three affluent bears who tried to burn her and drown her.

• In 1697, Charles Perrault published nine *Tales of My Mother Goose*, arguably the most popular work in all French literature. He trimmed some excesses from the original folk tales and added such details as Prince Charming and Cinderella's pumpkin coach.

• In 1992, a politically correct version of Hans Christian Andersen's stories was produced by Chronicle Books, a U.S. publisher, and promptly incensed Danes, who regard the author as a national treasure. Changes made or suggested included allowing the Little Match Girl to survive and altering "black magic" to "bad magic."

Canada's Napoleon?

On January 6, 1854, the world's first consulting detective, Sherlock Holmes, was born in North Riding, Yorkshire. A Canadian-born U.S. astronomer was the inspiration for Professor James Moriarty, the nemesis of Holmes and the "Napoleon of Crime," contends Bradley Schaefer, a U.S. space agency scientist. Simon Newcomb (1835-1909), born in Nova Scotia, was superintendent of the U.S. Nautical Almanac Office and that country's most prominent astronomer in the past century. Sir Arthur Conan Doyle, creator of Holmes, heard about Mr. Newcomb through an astronomer friend, Col. Alfred Drayson, Mr. Schaefer believes. According to the *Boston Globe*, "Moriarty and Newcomb, for example, were both mathematical geniuses who published papers on the binomial theorem at the age of 20 and later wrote about the orbits of asteroids. They were professors of mathematics at small universities until forced to resign. Their leadership was based on repeated successes, intimidating personalities and the fear of their associates."

Regrets? I've had a few

Thomas Gilovich, a psychologist at Cornell University, is a pioneer in the field of regret study, says the *New York Times*. In examining the relationship of regret to sex, he has found only one sharp sex-based contrast. "Men were far more likely to say, 'I regret not sleeping with that woman,' while women said, 'I regret sleeping with that man.'"

Significant digits

• Two-thirds: Two-thirds of the planet's original forests have been felled, says the Washington-based Worldwatch Institute. Forests once covered 34 per cent of the Earth's land.

• One: Virtually everyone in the United States gets at least a mild case of food poisoning each year, according to the *Los Angeles Times*.

• Two: Just 2 per cent of people are cheerful every day and 5 per cent have bad moods on four of five days.

• Two to ten: According to David Richardson, a British scientist with the food conglomerate Nestle, "The consumption of half a can (200 grams) of baked beans a day in a normal healthy diet can increase flatus production by more than two to ten times the amounts produced on a fibre-free diet."

• Three: A "standard human male" at rest needs one Mars bar of energy every three hours, according to Dr. Charles

Ellington, writing in *Nature*. Jogging or manual work pushes this to one bar an hour. The equivalent energy consumption of a bumblebee, measured by its breathing, is a Mars bar every 30 seconds.

• 19: Nineteen out of 20 businesses in Canada and the United States are either owned or controlled by families.

• 20 to 50: Lefties make up 20 to 50 per cent of people with speech defects and about 25 per cent of all deaf people. Roughly 40 per cent of the mentally handicapped are southpaws. A disproportionate number of reporters, editors, and broadcasters are left-handed, according to a 1984 survey.

• 32: "Roughly every month, somewhere above the Earth, there is an explosion the size of the Hiroshima bomb, caused by meteorites striking the atmosphere and being burned up by it," writes Adrian Berry in the *Daily Telegraph*. The explosions, which tend to occur 32 kilometres above the planet, have been observed since 1975 by secret military satellites looking for nuclear attacks.

• 35: Although it is associated with the very old, Alzheimer's is found in some families as early as age 35, says the *Miami Herald*.

• 39: A low opinion of "Wisian-Americans" is held by 39 per cent of Americans, according to the 1989 General Social Survey. There are no such people.

• 1,000: In 1993, about 1,000 new books were printed in English every day. Today's major libraries double in size every 14 years.

• 500,000: Helena Cronin, a British researcher in evolutionary theory, is convinced that chimpanzees exhibit consciousness – rather than just unconscious instinct – because "a mere 500,000 generations" separate humankind from apekind.

• One million: Wooden shoes are still used by about a million

Dutch farmers, factory workers, and fishermen. They are dry and environmentally sound and do not collapse when a cow steps on them.

World o' names

• In piercing jargon, a hole drilled right between the eyes at the bridge of the nose is called "Earl," says the *Los Angeles Times*. It is named for Earl Van Aken, an Orange County fitness instructor who was among the first to ask for it.
• Anne Rice, the gothic novelist who has written books such as *Interview with the Vampire*, was born Howard Allen O'Brien in 1941. (She changed her first name to Anne before marrying Stan Rice.)
• Zane Grey, the author of such rugged tales of the old west as *Riders of the Purple Sage*, was born Pearl Grey. He dropped his given name when he began to write professionally.
• In Denmark, authorities consider "Kim" a masculine name, despite the obvious existence of Kim Basinger.

Counterfeiters' wiles

On January 11, 1815, Sir John A. Macdonald was born. Canada's first prime minister can be seen on the $10 bill; if he's winking, it's a counterfeit. Authorities have had a long battle of wits with forgers. Some reports from *Globe* files:
• 1939: Toronto police warn that someone is silvering Jamaican pennies and passing them off as Canadian and U.S. 50-cent pieces.
• 1940: Higher-denomination counterfeit bills are tougher to fob off, writes New York criminologist Carleton Simon in *The Canadian Police Gazette*, adding, "there are many people who

seldom possess a $20 bill because of their economic circum-
stances." A U.S. counterfeiter, George Brown (no relation to
the *Globe*'s first publisher), was among the first to use photography in making bogus bills and could also peel a genuine bill
in half to double his money, Dr. Simon says.

• 1946: If you run a suspect $5 bill over your earlobe, says
Toronto engraver A. E. MacNutt, and compare it with a
genuine note, any difference in texture will show its bogus
nature.

• 1949: In Vancouver, 66-year-old engraver Ernest Conduit is
kidnapped and held for five days as crooks try to persuade him
to create a plate for a bogus $20 bill. He persuades them he
could not do it himself.

• 1950: British police investigate the labels on crates of Spanish
oranges. They look so much like one-pound notes, says
Reuters, that one was actually passed in a London bar.

• 1961: Teenagers in Grimsby, Ontario, are caught dropping
pennies into nitric acid, wearing them down to the size of
dimes, and using them to buy cigarettes.

• 1973: A gas-station attendant in Brandon, Manitoba, realizes
he has accepted a bogus $100 bill; the portrait of the Queen
has been replaced by a chinchilla.

A measure of rulers

January 16, 1547, saw the crowning of Russia's first czar, Ivan
the Terrible. Rulers of the past were often given bynames that
revealed their attributes or characters. Some examples:

• Top drawer: Ferdinand the Desired, John the Perfect Prince,
James the Conqueror, Elizabeth the Virgin Queen, Edmund
the Deed-Doer, John the Fearless, and many rulers called
"great," "good," or "wise."

• Above average: Philip the Handsome, Peter the Ceremonious, John the Steadfast, Ferdinand the Benign, Louis the Lion, Robert the Pious, and Louis the Debonair.
• So-so: Philip the Fair, Louis from Overseas, Charles the Well-Beloved (a.k.a. Charles the Mad), Ferdinand the Fickle, and Henry the Liberal.
• Getting personal: Louis the Blind, Charles the Bald, Michael the Drunkard, John the Redhead, Henry the Impotent, Charles the Lame, Henry the Fat, Louis the Stammerer, Louis the Stubborn, and William the Silent.
• Wimps: Edward the Confessor, Rudolph the Sluggard, Henry the Sufferer, Charles the Simple, and Louis the Do-Nothing.
• Definite pans: William the Bad, Pedro the Cruel, Henry the Fratricide, John the Posthumous, and Robert the Devil. (Source: *Encyclopedia Britannica*.)

Thesaurus rex

On January 18, 1779, thesaurus-compiler Peter Mark Roget was born, emerged, arrived, appeared, was introduced, debuted, had his beginning, was presented, burst forth, came into the world, first saw the light of day, made a break for it, got going.

Go whistle for it

Chances are, some idiot is whistling today – not in a news-room or a theatre, one hopes, because the irritating habit, which sets nerves on edge, is considered bad luck. A few sibilant notes:
• Earlier in this century, street-corner whistling mirrored popular music. Old-time performers who whistled as part of

their acts include Bing Crosby, Al Jolson, Sammy Davis, Jr., Jack Benny, and Pete Seeger.

• There are jazz whistlers and classical whistlers.

• Most whistlers blow; some suck. Classical whistlers are classified by range and quality of tone. They include sopranos and coloraturas. A two-octave range is considered good.

• Gomera, one of the Canary Islands, is famous for its whistling language, *silbo gomero*. The skill was apparently taught to the current inhabitants by the extinct, aboriginal Guanche people – who may have been of Cro-Magnon origin. Whistling and simultaneously articulating, islanders can reproduce anything that can be said in Spanish; a waitress can relay a café order, doctors can be alerted within minutes of a medical emergency, and many people in outlying areas can dodge the tax collector because they have been warned that he is coming.

• Superstitions: whistling inside a house is as risky as opening an umbrella indoors; whistling aboard a ship summons up a gale.

• In 1981, a study of airplane voice-recorder tapes taken from accidents found that 80 per cent of the pilots involved did some whistling in the last half-hour of flight.

Thank you, science

In January 1993, the *New York Times* announced that Joseph Weintraub of that city had created a computer program, PC Professor, that "creates the illusion of an opinionated person."

The burden of beasts

On January 25, 1993, revellers in Manganeses de la Polvorosa, Spain, attacked a British animal lover who objected to their custom of "Tossing the She Goat" – dropping an animal out of a church tower into a tarpaulin. (Twice in the previous five years, goats died when they missed the canvas.) The town's fiesta was perhaps the most notorious of Spain's 300 celebrations that involved cruelty to animals – they can include decapitation of hanging birds, driving cattle into the sea, or stoning small birds and animals to death. Spanish and foreign animal lovers always want to curb such rituals, which may be pagan holdovers. However, the early Christian era also meant hard times for Europe's animals:

• Citing the Bible, officials tried harmful domestic animals in criminal courts; wild beasts fell under the jurisdiction of ecclesiastical courts and, if found guilty, were banished and exorcised.

• In France alone, 92 trials of animals occurred between 1120 and 1740, when a cow was executed.

• One of the first trials occurred in AD 864, when it was decreed in Germany that a swarm of bees that had stung a man to death should be suffocated. (In 11th-century France, St. Bernard excommunicated a swarm of bluebottles that annoyed him while he was preaching.)

• Lawyers and clergy profited by the rigmaroles. In 1445, for instance, the commune of St. Julien launched a lawsuit against beetles. After 42 years, a compromise settlement was proposed, but a legal snag was discovered that restarted the case. In 1521, French lawyer Bartholomew Chassenee made his reputation by defending a pack of rats and having charges dropped.

• Domestic animals could be character witnesses in 17th-century Savoy if their owners were charged with murder.

• Swine roamed freely in France; one was hanged in 1394 in Normandy for eating a child. In 1547, a sow was executed for a similar crime, but her six piglets were treated as young offenders and spared.

• The Swiss often prosecuted worms for destroying crops. In 1451, a number of leeches were hauled into court in Lausanne and ordered to leave the district within three days. In 1659, Italians charged caterpillars with trespassing.

• In 1471, a rooster in Basel laid an egg; both were burned at the stake.

• In 1499, the trial of a rampaging German bear was delayed when defence counsel argued for a jury of its peers.

• As recently as 1906, two Swiss brothers and their dog were tried for murder: the men got life sentences; the dog was executed.

Medical watch

• Since 1987, gerontologists at the University of Southern California have been studying 200 master athletes – people 40 and older who compete in at least one sanctioned event annually. Their oldest subject is Jack Bishin, 91, who can cover five kilometres on foot in 40 to 50 minutes.

• When dieting, it helps to visualize the weight you want to lose as butter, says the *Dallas Morning News*. A pound of butter is roughly equal in size to a pound of fat.

Eine kleine debunking

On January 27, Wolfgang Mozart (1756-91) was born. By all accounts, Mozart was short and perpetually sickly, very thin and pale with a mop of pale hair. Yet, he was said to be able to cast a spell on any woman with his eyes. Contrary to rumour, he was not poisoned. Contemporary research concludes Mozart probably died of the effects of a blood-letting administered to counter acute rheumatic fever. He wasn't really named Amadeus and only used that name in humorous letters to his family. His baptismal names were Johannes Chrysostomos Wolfgangus Theophilus. ("Amadeus" and "Theophilus" both mean "loved by God.") Mozart's income during the final eight years of his life was 3,000 to 4,000 florins – somewhere between $90,000 and $120,000 in today's currency. He and his wife Constanze lived grandly, employing two servants. Mozart was heavily indebted when he died because he gambled and he and his wife spent money as fast as he earned it.

Costs of sloughing off

Some of the effects of the annual fitness slump from January to April, according to *Longevity* magazine:
- What goes first: good moods.
- What lasts longest: flexibility.
- How long it takes to lose fitness: three to six weeks.
- How long it takes to get it back: eight to ten weeks.
- Minimum weight gain: about three pounds.
- What makes stops/starts harder on the body: getting older.
- Best slump prevention: cut workouts by up to two-thirds, but don't stop entirely.

Curiouser and curiouser

On January 27, 1832, Charles Lutwidge (Lewis Carroll) Dodgson was born. Any other date is one of his unbirthdays. Some notes about a man who once winged a story to amuse a few children and thus created the third-most-quoted book in English, after the Bible and Shakespeare's works:

• Charles Lutwidge Dodgson was a shy mathematics professor at Oxford. Dealing with adults, he had a bad stammer; with children, especially little girls, he was more relaxed.

• In July 1862, Dodgson and a friend, Robinson Duckworth, took Alice Liddell and her two sisters for a picnic on the Thames. The author began a fairy tale. (Mr. Duckworth said, "I remember turning around and saying, 'Dodgson, is this an extempore romance of yours?' And he replied, 'Yes, I'm inventing it as we go along.'")

• At the end of the day, Alice, ten, asked Dodgson to write down his story. He did so, and thought nothing more of it. Henry Kingsley, a novelist visiting the Liddells, chanced upon *Alice's Adventures Underground* and urged the family to persuade Dodgson to publish.

• The author expanded the work into *Alice's Adventures in Wonderland* and devised his pseudonym: he translated his given names into Latin, switched their order, and turned them back into English.

• By the time of Dodgson's death in 1898, *Alice* – comprising Wonderland and a second tale, *Through the Looking Glass* – was the most popular children's book in England. Eventually, it was one of the most popular in the world.

• Alice has been translated into 75 languages; one U.S. collector has more than 1,000 different editions. There are almost a dozen film versions of *Alice in Wonderland*.

• One of Dodgson's hobbies was portrait photography, sometimes little girls in the nude. Defenders say this was a fad of the times and the author – a lifelong bachelor – was too religious and innocent to have meant anything by it. At some point, the Liddell family broke off relations with Dodgson and burned his letters to Alice. However, all his "child friends" spoke well of him and Alice Liddell asked him to be the godfather of her first child.

• In 1880, Dodgson abruptly gave up photography. In 1890, he issued a pamphlet denying any connection with Lewis Carroll, although he had autographed dozens – perhaps hundreds – of the early books. Towards the end of his life, mail addressed to Lewis Carroll was returned to the post office marked "Unknown."

The tabloids say ...

• Adolf Hitler reborn – and sues for slander (*Weekly World News*).
• Ouch! Pooch gets grip on a flasher (*National Examiner*).
• Never mind a coffee break, wave of the future at office is a sex break (*Star*).
• Husband's bean diet gave me lung cancer (*Sun*).
• Man drives away pesky gophers with rock music (*National Enquirer*).
• Grandmother, 67, still looks 22 – senior citizen discounts hard to get, she says (*Sun*).
• Penguin stampede kills seven men in Antarctica (*Weekly World News*).

Thought du month

"If you do not think about the future you cannot have one." – British novelist and playwright John Galsworthy (1867-1933) in *Swan Song*.

February

Winter: How long?

The length of winter varies at different points in Canada. If the season is measured from the first snow cover of one inch (2.54 centimetres) or more until the last one-inch snow cover, winter lasts 291 days in Resolute, Northwest Territories – 80 per cent of the year. The shortest winters are in B.C. communities such as Estevan Point (25 days) and Victoria (53) days.

Drop that shovel

"If you wanted to design an absolutely perfect act to damage the joints and discs in the lower back, you'd have to compress the spine – like you do when you're lifting – and rotate, and that's just what shovelling is," says Dr. Lee Magenheim of New York.

Brushing up on tooth care

On February 2, 1709, Alexander Selkirk was rescued. The cast-
away, who was the inspiration for Robinson Crusoe, had been
marooned on an island for four years. That's a long time to go
without a toothbrush:

• The first brush, used by the ancients, was the
"chew stick" – a pencil-sized stick with one
end frayed to a soft, fibrous condition.
Examples have been found in Egyptian
tombs dating to 3000 BC.

• Chew sticks are still used in remote parts of the world, such
as the U.S. South. Rubbed on the teeth, they can be as effective as modern nylon-bristle brushes. Dentists have reported
on one elderly man in Shreveport, Louisiana, who used frayed
white-elm sticks all his life; he had plaque-free teeth and
healthy gums.

• The modern bristle toothbrush originated in China in 1498.
When traders brought the hogs'-bristle-and-bamboo brushes
to Europe, they were unpopular because they were too firm.
Europeans substituted horse-hair brushes; in 1723, a French
dentist criticized these for being too soft.

• By the turn of the century, natural-bristle brushes were so
expensive that U.S. families would share one. Boarding houses
and college dorms used communal brushes. (As recently as
1980, just one out of every three Americans owned a toothbrush. The rest shared.)

• In 1938, Du Pont revolutionized the market with the first
nylon-bristle brushes. By the 1950s, the company had per-
fected a "soft" brush that was easier on the gums.

• Dentifrices, to clean teeth by adding a bit of abrasiveness,
have been made from ground-up coral, burnt eggshell, or

porcelain. Modern toothpaste contains ten or more ingredients; chalk is the main element. The worst products were probably the tooth powders made around the turn of the century: manufacturers congealed their ingredients into sticky paste by using honey or glucose syrup.

• Some people squeeze the middle of the tube; others roll up the end. In 1954, a Danish couple was granted a divorce after arguing over these two approaches. (Sources: Charles Panati's *Extraordinary Origins of Everyday Things*, news services.)

Grapefruit league

Spring-training usually begins this month. Baseball superstitions certainly do:

• Former Cardinals first baseman Orlando Cepeda believed there was only one hit in a bat. After he got a hit, he would discard his bat.

• Frank Chance, with the Cubs and Yankees from 1898 to 1914, would sleep only in a rail car's berth No. 13; if forced to accept another, he would write "13" on it.

• Arthur (Six o'Clock) Weaver, who played in the first decade of this century, would avoid tempting fate by abruptly leaving the field and heading home if the clock struck 6 P.M. during a game.

• Player/manager Leo Durocher would not change his clothes during a winning streak; he would also ride in the back of the bus during a losing streak.

• One day in the 1920s, Al Simmons of the Philadelphia Athletics was in such a hitting slump that he absentmindedly got out of his postgame shower and put on his fedora. Teammates laughed at the sight of the stunned player. The next day, Simmons got four hits. Before long, the Philadelphia clubhouse was full of naked men, dripping wet and wearing their fedoras. (Sources: *St. Louis Post-Dispatch*, *USAir* magazine, *Peanuts and Crackerjack*.)

The worth of a dollar

On February 4, 1986, the Canadian dollar reached a historic low of 69.13 cents (U.S.). Its highest value occurred during the U.S. civil war, 1861-65, when it rose to $1.45; at that time, Washington adopted the paper "greenback," causing some unhappy memories of the worthless "continental."

Utopian dreams

February 7 is the birthday of Sir Thomas More (1477-1535). In 1516, he wrote about an imaginary island off the shore of South America that he called "Utopia" – Greek for "no place." The inhabitants of this ideal world lived in 54 identical towns, gardened, devoted their spare time to learning, and dressed in black. Once a month, all wives had to kneel down in front of their husbands and beg forgiveness. The concept of an ideal society is much older than this English statesman's book:
• There were Norse, Celtic, and Arab legends of earthly paradises thought to lie somewhere to the west across the Atlantic Ocean.
• Plato's Republic describes a society ruled by philosopher-kings. There would be rigid censorship, no music or poetry, no families or marriages.
• Early socialists were frequently called utopians. They created concepts such as "industrialization" and the principle "From each according to his ability, to each according to his need."
• Between 1663 and 1858, about 140 utopian settlements were

founded in North America. Most were religious colonies. They tended to flourish during the lifetime of the leader – thought to have the gift of prophecy or wisdom – and then die away. However, groups such as the Hutterites still thrive.

• Some utopias practised celibacy; others, such as the Oneida Community in New England, had "complex marriage" with all husbands and wives being shared to dissolve selfishness.

• By the late 19th century, the utopian impulse had almost run its course in North America.

• There are at least four Utopias on the map: in Australia, Alaska, Texas, and outside Barrie, Ontario.

• The utopian novel *Walden Two*, written in 1948 by psychologist B. F. Skinner, inspired many hippie communes of the 1960s. A year after it was written, George Orwell published *1984*, a "dystopian" novel that describes the opposite of a utopia.

• In the 1970s, Cambodia's Khmer Rouge killed people who didn't fit into its utopian-communist society. Death was meted out for misdeeds such as falling asleep, playing the wrong music, or asking questions.

No reflection?

In February 1992, 21 of the world's top thinkers met behind closed doors at UNESCO headquarters in Paris. After two days of discussing the world's problems, the Ad Hoc Reflection Committee voted to say nothing. French philosopher and historian Michael Serres told the media, "Not saying anything can mean two things: either that we don't have anything to say or, on the contrary, that we have a lot to say."

Haley and Halley

February 9 is the anniversary of the death in 1981 of rock 'n' roller William John Clifton – known as Bill Haley, leader of the Comets. Also on this date, in 1986, Halley's Comet returned to view for the first time in 76 years. A comparison of the man and the comet:

• Bill Haley's song "Rock Around the Clock," released in 1954, became a hit a year later – making rock a mainstream social influence and wrecking a few theatres showing the film *Blackboard Jungle*, which featured the song in its opening sequence. It is one of the top-selling songs of all time. Halley's Comet, whose return was detected in 1985, reached its greatest prominence a year later. One of the brightest comets, it has caused fear and dismay in previous visits. In 1910, for example, a few people who feared the end of the world committed suicide and a virgin sacrifice was attempted in Oklahoma.

• The comet was a traditional harbinger of disaster. Bill Haley was the harbinger of rock music.

• Bill Haley was a white musician with greasy black hair. Halley's Comet is a ball of cosmic snow with a velvet-black nucleus.

• Halley's Comet is remembered in Britain because it appeared in 1066, before the Battle of Hastings. Bill Haley's career declined into obscurity except in Britain, where he appeared as recently as 1976.

• Bill Haley was cremated. Halley's Comet will eventually "burn up."

Word watch

• Dude: In 1990, U.S. soldiers in the Middle East were being cautioned not to use the phrase "Hey, dude," because "dude" is Arabic for worm.

• Um: a pause word in English that some people use more than 1,000 times an hour, according to psychologist Nicholas Christenfeld with the University of California. Foreign equivalents, says writer Joy Aschenbach, include *znachit* (Russian), *oder* or *nicht* (German), *hace* (Spanish), *nah* (Javanese), and *ondan sonra efendim* (Turkish).

• Etaerio: "an aggregate fruit," such as a strawberry. This word is termed "the meat and drink of the average Scrabble game," by professional player Phil Appleby of Britain. Leftover vowels can be a problem in Scrabble, at least in English-language play.

Valentine's Day

The wife of P. G. Wodehouse (1881-1975) got a love letter on her breakfast tray every morning – not just on February 14. Her husband, the British-born humour writer, was a good egg. Notes about other love missives:

• Between the 1790s and 1840s, vicious valentines were popular in Britain, writes Dalya Alberge in the *Independent*. When the penny-post mail service was introduced and it was the recipient who paid the postage, fathers of injured daughters demanded refunds on the unpleasant cards. Between 1797 and 1800, there were thousands of such requests.

• In December 1993, one of Mozart's letters to his father was auctioned by Sotheby's. In it, the composer denies that he is having an affair with Constanze, his lover and wife-to-be.

On the other side of the scrap of paper is the handwriting of Constanze.

• Also in 1993, a letter from Inessa Armand, Lenin's disciple and translator in Paris, was discovered in Moscow archives. The daughter of a Russian actor, a feminist and an early Bolshevik, Ms. Armand had previously caused a scandal by running off with her 18-year-old brother-in-law after the birth of her fourth son. In her letter to Lenin, she ends with, "I kiss you over and over," says the *Times* of London. By contrast, the Communist love god usually ended his letters to her with the closing remark, "I give you a firm handshake." When she died in 1920, she was buried in Red Square. Lenin showed rare emotion at her funeral, leaning on his wife, Nadezhda Krupskaya, for support.

• In 1992, lawyer Jay Rothman of Tarzana, California, sued a flower shop that misplaced the love letter he intended to accompany a bouquet of flowers to his wife. "I'm a hard-nosed, aggressive plaintiff's attorney," he said. Writing the note was "one of the only times in my life that I was really inspired."

Pluto discovered

On February 18, 1930, U.S. astronomer Clyde Tombaugh discovered Pluto. In 1991, the 85-year-old recalled how the planet was named: "All the planets are named after mythological deities, but by 1930 a lot of the names had already been used on asteroids. Only three names for the new planet were seriously considered: Minerva, Cronus, and Pluto. Minerva was at first the most popular choice but, sure enough, it had already been used on an asteroid. Cronus was suggested by a certain egotistical and widely disliked astronomer, so Pluto became the unanimous choice of the [observatory] staff."

Proper names

• In February 1994, Beatrice and Helmut Heiber published *Die Reuckseite des Hakenkreuzes* (The Other Side of the Swastika), describing everyday life in Nazi Germany. One chapter describes how officials protected the "Hitler" name, denying its use for tarts, church bells, mountains, and roses. (One small town did get permission to call itself Hitler Heights.) Parents were allowed to name their daughters "Adolfine" but not "Hitlerine."
• In 1972, Joseph Desire chose the Africanized title "Mobutu Sese Seko Koko Ngbendu Waza Banga" when he became absolute ruler of Zaire. It means "the all-powerful warrior who, because of endurance and an inflexible will to win, will go from conquest to conquest leaving fire in his wake."

Significant digits

• 1.5: About 99.99 per cent of all pesticides in the human diet are natural substances produced by plants, according to Bruce Ames, director of the Environmental Health Sciences Centre at Berkeley, California. People eat an estimated 1.5 grams a day of natural pesticides; there are 5,000 to 10,000 of them.
• One: About 1 per cent of all words spoken in the United States are profane, estimates Timothy Jay, a Massachusetts psychologist and author of *Cursing in America*. He calculates that, in a five-minute exchange at normal speed, conversationalists will utter three swear words.
• Two: "The odds of a drifting object making it across the Pacific Ocean," writes Lisa Schnellinger of Hearst News Service, "are greater than one might expect – about 2 per cent."
• Two to three: People concerned about getting enough water

every day "need to be sensitive to their own bodies and their ways," contends U.S. nutrition consultant Christine Palumbo. "The keys are frequency and colour of urination. You want to urinate every two to three hours with a good stream and a light-yellow colour, the shade of lemon juice."

• Three: After a year of jumping up and down, middle-aged women taking part in a study by the University of Nottingham "had increased their hip-bone density by 3 per cent as well as stimulating bone formation," reports the *New Scientist*. Researchers said that women should do 50 jumps a day to help stave off osteoporosis because the ground impact is an important factor in triggering bone formation.

• Five: About 5 per cent of the population never gets a cold, according to doctor-columnist Art Mollen. This has been linked to greater innate immunity as a result of good genes.

• Seven: By a "relatively exact" estimate, says the *Dallas Morning News*, one of every seven people on the planet can communicate in English.

• 7.5: In 19th-century Europe, tattooing became popular among aristocrats when the tomb of a tattooed Egyptian princess was discovered. In 1880, the *New York Times* reported, "at least 7.5 per cent of fashionable London ladies are tattooed in inaccessible localities."

• 16: During 1970-88, William Hartman of the Centre for Marital and Sexual Studies in California made laboratory studies of the orgasms of 469 women and 289 men. The largest number of orgasms recorded for a man was 16 an hour and for a woman 134 an hour. (He claims that 12 per cent of men have the potential for multiple orgasms.)

• 35: From Florida's *Image* magazine: "You can fit as much as $1 million into an average suitcase and it will weigh perhaps 35 pounds."

• 37: If you imagine the age of the Earth as 12 hours, the human race is 37 seconds old and fish 80 minutes.

• 59: The average age for seeking help for impotence is 59, according to U.S. urologists. They estimate that half the men they treat have waited for two years before making an appointment and some have waited as long as ten.

• 60: Among adult Americans finished with schooling, nearly 60 per cent have never read a single book and most of the rest read only one book a year, says Alvin Kernan, author of *The Death of Literature*.

• 70: In 1993, a British woman was discovered to have kept her blindness secret for 70 years from her family, says the *Daily Mirror*. The husband of Rose Northmore, who was 72, finally discovered her secret when she asked him to buy her a "talking book." He took her to a doctor, who said she had only 1.5 per cent of normal vision. "I was stunned," said Norman Northmore. "We had been married 48 years and I had no idea." Mrs. Northmore explained, "I didn't want to bother anyone."

• 2,213: In 1990, the Ontario Mining Association stated, "Take the CN Tower and turn it upside down. Stick it into the ground and drive three more CN Towers on top of it. The point of the bottom tower would be 2,213 metres below the surface. We have miners working at those depths in Ontario."

• 100 million: In an average year, 100 million people worldwide come down with the flu.

Second sight? Again?

In February 1828, Sir Walter Scott wrote in his diary that he was being strangely haunted by a "sense of pre-existence." The preceding day at dinner, says *The Chambers Book of Days* (1863), he was nagged by a feeling "that the same topics had been discussed, and the same persons had stated the same opinions on them." The prolific author described the mental condition as resembling a mirage in the desert. We might call it *déjà vu*:

• In 1886, German psychiatrist Emil Kraepelin introduced the word "paramnesia" to describe errors of memory. One of the varieties was *paramnesia tout court*, or *déjà vu* – a curious sense of extreme familiarity.

• *Déjà vu* has aroused considerable interest, says the *Encyclopedia Britannica*, and is occasionally felt by most people, especially in youth or when they are fatigued. The feeling may be confined to a single sense, such as hearing, but is usually generalized and includes a subject's own actions.

• As a rule, *déjà vu* passes away in a few seconds or minutes. However, in some epileptics, the condition lasts for hours or even days.

• *Déjà vu* is well-known among creative types. Sir Walter, writer of dozens of books and editor of 70 volumes, had been "breaking himself down by over-hard literary work," says Mr. Chambers. Other authors who have noted the condition include Shelley, Dickens, Hawthorne, Tolstoy, and Proust.

• Plato believed *déjà vu* to be evidence of reincarnation. Other explanations: partly forgotten memory or fantasy; a hypnosis-like trance; epilepsy, especially of the right temporal lobe; precognition (seeing things before they occur – known to the Scottish as "second sight"); retrocognition (the supposed transmission of knowledge directly from one's ancestors); psychometry (picking up visions of the past from a material object).

• *Déjà vu* is a curious sense of extreme familiarity.

Medical watch

• In 1992, a "Churchill gene" that protects some people from heart disease despite their unhealthy lifestyles was being sought by British scientists. The wartime leader, who died at 90, consumed an estimated 22 units of alcohol a day, smoked huge numbers of cigars, was short, overweight and aggressive, and had been a premature baby – all cardiac risk factors.

• Our brains were never intended to last as long as they do, contends Gary Lynch, a University of California neuroscientist. "If you take animals in the wild, they don't live even 25 per cent of their potential maximum life span."

• During sleep, the sympathetic nervous system – which prepares the body for emergencies – can be twice as active as is normal when people are awake. "Even at four in the morning, when you think the body should be fast asleep and quiet, everything is pounding away," said Dr. Virend Somers of the University of Iowa.

• In February 1994, 102-year-old Charles Fletcher of Nottinghamshire, England, was given a heart pacemaker. "It is proving to be a real boon to me," said the former factory designer, who was wounded and left for dead in the First World War and who was still attending his regiment's reunions.

• Contestants in beauty pageants should carry Preparation H, writes Karen Heller in *The Philadelphia Inquirer Magazine*. The product can be used to tone thighs and also "works wonders in eliminating bags under eyes."

• In pre-Hispanic times, natives of the Americas used hallucinogenic enemas, in some cases to commune with their ancestors.

• A few people (more commonly women) have structural flaws in their skulls, reports the *Lancet*, and can lose brain fluids when they blow their noses enthusiastically.

The tabloids say ...

• Loyal dog digs up dead master's body and drags him home (*Weekly World News*).
• Woman cured of throat cancer after licking Elvis stamp (*Sun*).
• Revealed! Martha Raye's sex secrets (*Globe*).
• Snoring dad suffocates as tot stuffs crayons up his nose (*Sun*).
• Lawyers would rather write bestsellers (*Star*).
• Dad restores son's ability to speak – by shooting at him (*Sun*).
• Woman wants to be blind again – 'cause men are too ugly (*Weekly World News*).

Thought du month

"Our company had a meeting to discuss the recession, and we voted not to have one!" – professional U.S. motivator Zig Ziglar.

M a r c h

The British invasion

On March 2, 1963, the Beatles first reached No. 1 on the British hit parade with "Please, Please Me." However, a U.S. executive with Capitol Records told the group's producer, "They won't do anything in this market." At that time, the giant U.S. record market was tough for British artists to crack. An account of how the Beatles did it:

• In February 1963, "Please, Please Me" got its U.S. release on Vee Jay, a basically black label, and was attributed to the "Beetles." (In July, the group's first album was released; only 600 to 700 copies moved.)

• In the fall, "She Loves You" became a British million-seller. Released in the United States, it got sparse play. (However, the song "Love Me Do" was a Canadian hit and the Beatles' sound did filter across the border.)

• On October 17, the group recorded "I Want to Hold Your Hand." Manager Brian Epstein said, "Now we go and attack the States!"

• By November 1963, Beatlemania took hold in Britain. Still nothing in the United States.

• Television host Ed Sullivan, passing through London airport, got a taste of Beatlemania when the group returned from a tour. On December 10, a Beatles film clip aired on the CBS Evening News. A Washington disc jockey got a copy of "I Want to Hold Your Hand" via a British flight attendant and it was a hit.

• By late December, Beatlemania had caught hold in the United States. By April 4, 1964, Beatles songs held the top five spots on the Billboard Hot 100.

• TV host Jack Paar, who had seen the Beatles in person in November, showed a clip January 3, 1964, on his "Tonight Show" – the Beatles' first U.S. TV exposure. In February, they appeared twice on "The Ed Sullivan Show," scoring 73 million viewers on February 9.

• In August-September 1964, the group had a tumultuous tour of 25 U.S. and Canadian cities. They were young men in their early 20s, with a 28-year-old manager, "neolithic hairdos," and Liverpudlian "braying."

• Adults' reaction: "They are, apparently, part of some kind of malicious, bilateral entertainment trade agreement." – the *Washington Post*. "You can figure it this way – that's 16,000 kids who aren't out stealing hubcaps." – a San Francisco cop.

• Young people's reaction: For the most part, "Eeeeeeeeeee!"

• The Beatles were clever enough to be honest, refusing to deny they smoked and drank. They began the rock tradition of bantering with the media. (What do you do with your long hair in the shower? Ringo: "Get it wet. Dry it with a towel. Rub it.")

• Returning from North America, the Beatles began their first feature film, tentatively titled *Beatlemania*. It was part of a three-picture deal, with all rights reverting to the producer in 15 years. "After all, what pop group would still be popular after 15 years?" thought Mr. Epstein. *A Hard Day's Night* was shot cheaply, quickly, in black and white, with very little plot. The art-film result drew raves from the intelligentsia. (Sources: *Globe* files, *Rock of Ages*, *The Love You Make*, and *Beatles '64: A Hard Day's Night in America*.)

World o' music

Canada is the sixth-largest market for music; globally, the industry was worth about $39 billion in 1992. The top ten markets for recordings, says the *European*, are: the United States (31.1 per cent of world sales), Japan (15.2 per cent), Germany (9.2), Britain (7.0), France (6.8), Canada (3.0), Italy and the Netherlands (both 2.3), Spain (2.0), and Australia (1.7).

See Dick run

On March 2, 1982, author Philip Dick died. He wrote *Do Androids Dream of Electric Sheep?* which was the basis for the classic science-fiction movie *Blade Runner* (1982). Some notes about the cult writer, described by some as a "brilliant, mystical visionary" and by others as a raving madman whose fantasies filled "an endless series of lumpily written" novels:

• Philip Kindred Dick and his twin sister Jane were born in Chicago in 1925. The premature infants were feeble; after six weeks, Jane was dead. Throughout his life, guilty about having hogged his mother's milk, Dick wrote to Jane in his journals and books.

• For a brief time, Dick went to college in Berkeley, California, where he hung out with beatniks and used drugs.

• From 1953 to 1982, Dick wrote three dozen science-fiction novels and several hundred short stories. Fuelled by amphetamines and occasional horsemeat from a pet shop, he was able to type 120 words a minute; in a two-year period, he wrote 11 novels. His works are full of speculation about the nature of reality and the mind.

• Dick had five marriages, three nervous breakdowns, several suicide attempts, and many love affairs. At various times, he believed the FBI, the CIA, the Black Panthers, his ex-wives, and a local easy-listening radio station were out to get him.

• In 1972, Mr. Dick went to Vancouver to attend a science-fiction convention. Initially, he liked Canada. During his two-month stay, he fell in love four times, attempted suicide, and managed to kick his amphetamine habit in a drug-recovery centre.

• By 1974, Dick came to believe he had dual consciousness and claimed he had been contacted by Valis, a godlike intelligence system (related to his dead sister) that told him the universe was a hologram and history was an illusion.

• Dick's lifestyle and writing have inspired a cult following, especially in Europe and Japan, which sees him as a drug-stoked prophet. Some devotees call themselves Dick Heads.

• In 1982, Dick suffered a series of strokes and died before seeing *Blade Runner*'s début. He was buried beside his twin sister. (Sources: *Divine Invasions*, the *Blade Runner* script, news services.)

Justifiable paranoia

In 1987, nurses at Holy Cross Hospital in Silver Springs, Maryland, were switching around the dial of an office TV set and found that their dressing room was live on Channel 16.

A booby-trapped nation

In March 1994, a fry cook in northern Portugal pulled a live hand-grenade from a sack of French potatoes. The local bomb squad, which detonated the device, said it had probably been harvested from a field and processed along with the spuds. Some notes:

• "Everywhere in France – in potato fields and orchards, under town squares and back porches – the fallout from two world wars has turned the national soil into an enormous booby trap," writes Donovan Webster in *Smithsonian* magazine.

• Authorities estimate there are 12 million unexploded shells from the first war in the Verdun region, millions more in battle zones along the Somme and Marne, and millions of explosive devices from the Second World War embedded in the beaches of Normandy and Brittany.

• The most widely used devices in the First World War, 75-mm shells, look like corroded hairspray cans. When picked up, some shells slosh with poisonous liquids that can burn hands or even kill if the casing is leaky.

• Civilians discover bombs, sometimes leaving them beside country lanes for pickup. In 1993, five chilly lumberjacks died on the steep hills of the Argonne Forest when they lit a bonfire and heated up a bomb just below the surface.

• Since 1946, more than 600 bomb-disposal experts (*demineurs*) have died while gathering tens of millions of explosive devices.

Authorities say it will take centuries for some bombs in French soil to work their way to the sunshine.

A near miss

On March 15, 1994, the Earth came the closest yet in recent times to an astronomical disaster, says the *Independent on Sunday*. An asteroid 20 metres across passed by the planet at a distance of between 160,000 and 180,000 kilometres – less than half the distance to the moon. Had it hit, its impact would have equalled 20 Hiroshima-sized atomic explosions. An asteroid 350 metres across would cause an explosion equal to all the world's nuclear arsenals. It is estimated there are 1,000 asteroids larger than one kilometre in diameter whose orbits cross that of Earth; most are candidates for eventual collision.

Some golfing language

The object of the game is usually to strike the ball squarely and not foozle it by hooking, slicing, topping, or baffing. The old clubs included three "woods" – the driver, brassie, and spoon (or baffy) – and a series of "irons" – the cleek, mid-iron, driving mashie, lofting mashie, jigger, niblick, and putter. The term "bogey," which nowadays means one over par, originally meant the number of strokes a good average player (the mythical Colonel Bogey) would take to complete a hole.

You must remember this

In March 1992, Stephen Curry of Minnesota wandered 260 kilometres to his childhood home and was recognized by an acquaintance; he had disappeared five weeks earlier after telling his wife he was going hunting. Some words about forgetting:

• There are four main kinds of memory loss: anterograde amnesia (patient can't remember what happened after the onset but can remember past events), retrograde amnesia (can't remember the events before onset; a common result of concussion), paramnesia (familiar memories are distorted), and fugue state (person loses his or her identity and may take up a new way of living in a new place). They are caused by physical damage or severe psychological shocks.

• In 1986, a Winnipeg man on his way to the bank to deposit an income-tax refund disappeared and later showed up in Calgary.

• In 1987, a dozen people in Quebec and New Brunswick, hit hard by shellfish poisoning, suffered chronic memory loss for months afterward. They could no longer easily remember objects shown them a short time before.

• In 1942, John Crosswhite of Enid, Oklahoma, disappeared during a business trip to St. Louis. For 37 years, he lived as John Cross until he suffered a stroke and remembered some of his original identity; his daughter, one of the nurses looking after him, phoned Enid and discovered his original family. His first wife – an 83-year-old who had had Mr. Crosswhite declared legally dead in 1940 – was not told of his existence for fear of upsetting her.

• In 1971, James McDonnell of Larchmount, New York, suffered head injuries in two automobile accidents; he later found himself in Philadelphia. On Christmas Eve 1985, he bumped his head again, looked up his wife in the Larchmount phone book, and called home.

• In 1986, a Chicago surgeon paused while sewing up a patient and asked, "Did I take out that gall bladder?" The nurse assured him he had done so; she was obliged to answer the question after each stitch. The doctor was suffering from "transient global amnesia," a rare shutdown of the memory cells (it can be triggered by stress, immersion in cold water, or even sexual activity) and, although puzzled, carried on fearlessly and was back to normal in 48 hours. (Sources: *Collier's Encyclopedia*, *Globe* files, *Did You Know?*)

A hard-times scheme

In the spring of 1935, during the Great Depression, the modern chain letter first appeared, in Denver, Colorado – proclaiming a Prosperity Club. Although authorities in North America and elsewhere have come to regard such pyramid letters as nuisances and criminal rackets (if they involve money or merchandise), letters still pop up occasionally, like crabgrass or crocuses. Some jottings:

• The mythic "original" chain letter was perhaps the Flanders' Chain of Good Luck, said to have been started by a U.S. army officer during the First World War. Money was not involved; a recipient had to mail a "magic seven" copies for good luck.

• "One of the most famous of all chain letters," wrote syndicated columnist George Stimpson in 1939, "purports to have been written by Jesus just before the Crucifixion and deposited by him beneath a stone at the foot of the Cross. The receiver of the letter is enjoined to send copies of it to ten others, on pain of misfortune and bad luck."

• The Denver letter asked a person to send a dime to five people listed; the ultimate payoff was said to be $1,562.50. By April 29, 1935, the city had hired 100 extra clerks and carriers to handle its mail load; there was talk of a breakdown of the postal service.

• The craze spread throughout the U.S. West. Print shops worked overtime to turn out bales of chain form-letters. Some employers banned talk of the letters during office hours. One state legislature, says author Joseph Bulgatz, considered passing a law making it illegal to break a chain, and U.S. post-master James Farley mildly observed that "it sells stamps."

• Some people manipulated the money chains by putting their own names at the top or by adding pseudonyms, to get more cash. Entrepreneurs opened "factories" to help letter writers for a fee.

• Instead of cash, some letters passed along a pint of liquor, a dishtowel, a bale of hay, wartime propaganda, or political con-tributions. There was a "good-riddance" chain ("shoot the guy at the top of the list") and chains promising sex partners. One woman used a chain to locate her long-lost husband.

• In August 1979, the police chief of Petrolia, Ontario, said a chain letter had become the "talk of the town" and he'd have to arrest half its 4,300 residents if his department decided to lay charges. (In 1981, six residents of Chilliwack, British Columbia, were fined up to $3,000 for a scheme in which indi-viduals paid $2,200 to become entitled to receive $17,000.)

Birds fly north ...

Spring is the season opener for many bird watchers. Some ornithological notes:

• The observation of live birds in their natural habit is a popular pastime and scien-tific sport that developed almost entirely in this century, according to the *Encyclopedia Britannica*. In the 19th century, almost all students of birds carried guns to knock down

unfamiliar specimens for examination. As binoculars improved, life got a lot easier for birds.

• Bird-watching first became popular in Britain, with the United States not far behind. The pastime then spread to northern Europe and the older countries of the British Commonwealth.

• Experienced birders can do a lot of their identifying by ear.

• "Birders" is an overlapping term with "bird watchers," who observe the birds' behaviour. Birders, however, have a special interest in adding to their lists of species sighted. In Britain, they are known as "twitchers" – a term they dislike – and there are paging services that rent beepers to alert them when a rare bird visits the British Isles.

• Occasionally, bird watchers themselves have been watched. In 1960, for instance, English psychologist Helen Ross tracked a covey of zoologists in the Norwegian Arctic and recorded their foul language. They were most vocal when relaxed and happy, she writes in *Discovery* magazine. "The words used were blasphemous rather than obscene, as is to be expected among the middle classes."

... People fly south

Sandra Brown of Chapel Hill, North Carolina, who runs fear-of-flying seminars for American Airlines, offers these tips for nervous passengers:

• People bothered by the surge at takeoff probably will feel it less towards the rear of the plane.

• Those afraid of heights should sit by a window and pull the shade down.

• Claustrophobic passengers should sit by the aisle, if possible;

they should avoid middle and third seats in three-deep seating areas.

• People bothered by turbulence should sit over or near the wing, because there's less bouncing there.

• Drink plenty of water; dehydration tends to increase nervousness.

• Bring lots of things to occupy yourself and take your watch off so you don't keep checking the time.

Medical watch

• The more children a woman has, the less likely she is to commit suicide, according to a study of one million women over 25 by the University of Tromso in Norway.

• After calling for any nearby help, a person suspecting a heart attack should try coughing vigorously to convert an irregular heartbeat to normal, says Dr. Carl Bartecchi, author of *Emergency Cardiac Maneuvers*. "It could buy you time to get to a phone."

• Medical specialization was carried to absurd lengths in ancient Egypt, writes Ira Rutkow in *Surgery: An Illustrated History*. For instance, around certain pharaohs and their courts virtually every organ or sickness acquired its own specialist. One royal personage had one physician for his right eye and another for his left eye. In the Old Kingdom, there was Iry, who was "keeper of the king's rectum," and Hesi-Re, a tooth specialist.

• If men nick themselves while shaving, they tend to blame the blade, according to razor-maker Gillette. If women suffer a nick, they blame themselves.

Harley Davidsen

In March 1993, a Norwegian motorcycle enthusiast had his name legally changed to Harley Davidsen. He wasn't allowed to call himself "Davidson" because there's a law against having a Swedish name.

Significant digits

• Two: People with heart disease more than double their risk of heart attacks when they become angry, and the danger lasts for two hours, say U.S. researchers.

• Four: Most people get hungry every four hours, if they've eaten reasonable meals.

• 13: In 1993, Shane Seyer, a 13-year-old in Topeka, Kansas, was ordered to pay child support after getting his 17-year-old babysitter pregnant.

• 14: Also in 1993, a 14-year-old girl in Belfast who lived on a diet of junk food had developed scurvy, said her physician. The condition, caused by a deficiency of vitamin C, is more commonly associated with pre-19th-century seamen.

• 28: In any given year, 28 per cent of adult Americans are suffering from mental disorders, say researchers who recently surveyed 20,000 men and women. "The figures may sound high at first," said Dr. Myrna Weissman, a psychiatric epidemiologist at Columbia University. "But they are very consistent with what has been found in less extensive studies. Just think about the people you know."

• 20: In any two-week period, 20 per cent of the world's population is sick or malnourished, according to the World Health Organization.

• 34: "Genes determine when or whether one's hair turns

grey," writes Ellen Blum Barishi in *Chicago Tribune* magazine, "with most whites often turning noticeably grey at age 34 and African Americans at about 44."

• 50: When Superman turned 50 in 1987, his hero image was upgraded. He was promoted to columnist from reporter.

• 65: Toronto's CN Tower is struck by lightning an average of 65 times a year. Professional golfer Lee Trevino has been struck on two separate occasions.

• 85: "Almost everything you do today will be forgotten in just a few weeks," writes John McCrone in *New Scientist*. "The ability to retrieve a memory decays exponentially, and after only a month more than 85 per cent of our experiences will have slipped beyond reach, unless boosted by artificial aids such as diaries and photographs."

• 160: When the wind is blowing at least 160 kilometres an hour, human beings have the unique ability to lean into the blast and, while keeping their legs straight, touch one hand to the ground.

The Ides of March

On March 15, 44 BC, Caesar came out second best in a struggle at the Senate with a gang of assassins. Even then, he was feisty: there was no *Et tu Brute?* "It's generally accepted that Caesar's dying words were the Greek *Kai su, teknon?* Romans of his class moved easily between Latin and Greek," Greg Row of The Queen's College, Oxford, writes in the *Guardian*. "But it's important to recognize that he was not asking, 'You too, my son?' The words *Kai su* – found in Greek comedy and on mosaics – mean 'Screw you!' and the *teknon* ('kid') just makes it fiercer."

This just in: I'm not dead

Arguably, the least influential soothsayer was John Partridge of London. In 1708, satirist Jonathan Swift (writing as Isaac Bickerstaff) forecast that the horoscope publisher would die on March 29 of a raging fever. On March 30, Swift circulated a pamphlet saying his "rival" had snuffed it. Partridge spent his remaining days unsuccessfully advising his public he was not dead.

The tabloids say . . .

• Secretary fired for being too happy (*Weekly World News*).
• God plucked me out of the gutter at 66 to be a lawyer (*Globe*).
• Hot new teen trend – helping others (*Star*).
• Flying swami sucked into jet engine (*Weekly World News*).
• Daily beer keeps cat alive for 42 years (*Sun*).
• Guys and gals – yes, there's a difference (*National Examiner*).
• Siamese twins arrested – for fighting each other (*Weekly World News*).

Thought du month

"The nicest thing about the promise of spring is that sooner or later she'll have to keep it." – Mark Beltaire, cited in *The Fitzhenry & Whiteside Book of Quotations*.

A p r i l

April First

Before 1911, Canadian census counts were done on April Fool's Day.

All Fools' Day

• April 1 is the day when people get messages to call Mr. Lyon (and are given the zoo's telephone number), Mr. Stiff (the morgue), or Ms. Flame (the fire hall). It may be a relic of a Roman festival – Cerealia, held at the beginning of April – commemorating the fool's errand of the Earth goddess Demeter (Ceres, in Greek) who tried to track down the screams of her daughter, who had been carried off to hell by Pluto.
• Hebrews believed Noah was fooled on April 1, by a dove, into thinking the flood had abated. Some Christians believed

the Crucifixion occurred April 1 after a mockery of a trial.

• In 1971, state-run French radio said the Common Market had decided to make traffic drive on the left side of the road, to encourage Britain to join; police in the French Alps had to flag down several drivers who started early.

• In 1976, CJAD in Montreal upset listeners with the news that the city was building a castle for the Queen.

• In 1991, the *Financial Times of London* was tricked into printing discoveries of an Egyptologist named "Batson D. Sealing."

No fooling

On April 1, 1946, a huge earthquake off Alaska created a tsunami that travelled to Hawaii. Although people were warned, they thought it was an April Fools' joke; 159 islanders died. At the best of times, some news strains one's credulity:

• In April 1993, people in Berkeley, California, who were having difficult relationships with their houses could benefit from the services of "environmental psychologist" Clare Cooper Marcus. For $100 an hour, she conducted a role-playing session in which a client voiced his or her anxieties and the house responded.

• Also that month, China was abandoning its respect for too-good-to-be-true model workers and their deeds. Examples included Iron Man Wang, who reportedly went swimming in a tank of concrete to prevent it from hardening after factory equipment broke down, and mine worker Wang Junsho, who supposedly studied Mao's works by the light of glowworms.

• In April 1992, lonely old people in Japan could pay $1,100 to rent entertainers who would pretend to be their families for three hours.

Daylight Saving Time

On the first Sunday in April, most Canadians will advance their clocks by an hour (Saskatchewan remains on one time year-round). "Daylight Saving Time" has been a controversial issue in this century:
• In the First World War, both sides went to "summer time" to conserve resources.
• Canadian municipalities that adopted DST set the period as they saw fit. On September 18, 1938, for example, conscientious travellers going from Toronto to Kingston would start off with their watches on DST, go back an hour at Cobourg, go ahead an hour at Trenton, switch back at Napanee, and return to DST at their destination.
• In 1948, Alberta passed a law prohibiting DST. Offenders could be fined $25 for being an hour faster than other Albertans.
• On September 30, 1963, Argentina ended its summer time after 17 years.
• In 1966, the United States went to DST on the first Sunday in April. (In 1973, the country "sprang forward" on January 6, to conserve oil.)
• In 1987, Canada decided to go on DST three weeks early, to match the U.S. times.

Bad baseball

It's baseball time. Major-league baseball teams this season are unlikely to equal the pitiful record of the 1899 Cleveland Spiders, who had 20 wins and 134 losses to wind up 84 games out of first place. Their plight was caused by their owners, who had another franchise that they favoured: the St. Louis Perfectos. When a Spider showed even minimal talent, says the *Cleveland Plain Dealer*, he was grabbed away to the Perfectos. The Cleveland team even lost its player-manager, undertaker Joe Quinn.

The bees of summer

"People don't give honey bees the credit they deserve," says Jed Shaner, a beekeeper in Swoope, Virginia. The creatures pollinate more than 90 cultivated crops in North America, valued at billions of dollars. A U.S. apiarist estimates that a third of that country's diet is dependent, in some way, on honey-bee pollination. This is the season when flowers bloom and the bees go to work, in appalling conditions:
• The bees literally work themselves to death in three to five weeks of gathering nectar and pollen. It takes 12 bees labouring their full lifetimes to produce one teaspoon of honey.
• The genitals of a male honey bee explode like a grenade inside the queen bee when she mates – once – with a drone, reports Adrian Forsyth in *A Natural History of Sex*. He falls away with an audible pop and is dead before he hits the ground. His hundreds of rivals in the swarm aren't even that lucky.

Hippity-hop, hippity-hop

Watch out. Easter is the season for bunnies:
• In 1939, a jackrabbit in Orillia attacked a man bending over to chop wood, ripping his trousers. The animal later chased a St. Bernard and kicked in a window of the man's house.

• In 1954, a ten-kilogram rabbit in Voghera, Italy, attacked the hunter who had wounded it, sending the man to hospital with bites and scratches.

• In 1977, the New York office of the ASPCA had a rabbit called Harvey, described as "cranky" after previous owners had mistreated it. Snubbing other rabbits and biting anyone who came close, it was kept on the premises as an "attack rabbit."

• In 1979, Jimmy Carter reportedly had to fend off an aggressive, swimming rabbit with a canoe paddle. An Associated Press story said the bunny hissed menacingly, flashed its teeth, and flared its nostrils at the U.S. president.

• In 1981, firemen in Bristol, England, were called in to rescue a dog trying to escape the clutches of a sex-crazed rabbit. The pet rabbit, called Bunger, was insatiable and "nothing is safe from him," said his owner, 14-year-old Eleanor Walsh, adding that all the local cats and dogs were terrified. "I will take him to the vet next week."

World o' viruses

On April 12, 1955, Dr. Jonas Salk announced his vaccine against poliomyelitis and became a hero. (The previous year, for example, the viral scourge of polio had attacked more than 8,000 Canadians, crippling the majority and killing 481.) But many other viruses remain to be conquered; viruses cause more sickness than anything else on earth, says Peter Radetsky in his book *The Invisible Invaders*. Viruses are literally everywhere, including the surface of this page. They may be the most successful form of life – if they are alive.

Blowing in the wind . . .

Spring brings zephyrs, and the kite-flyers come out to play. In the Orient, kites have had religious purposes such as warding off evil spirits at night. Historically, they also had military purposes such as carrying signal lanterns. In 200 BC, a Chinese general flew a kite over an enemy fort to figure how far he'd have to tunnel to get inside. In 1232, the Chinese used kites to drop leaflets on the invading Mongols; unfortunately, very few Mongols knew how to read. Marco Polo reported that the Chinese flew men on reconnaissance kites but only those who were "stupid or drunk" would climb on board.

. . . Butterflies in the wind

Experts estimate that hundreds of millions of Monarch butterflies spend the winter in Mexico. However, the creatures that leave Mexico in the spring are three generations removed from those that will make the return fall journey south. Some notes:

• Appearance. So great is the change when a butterfly breaks out of its chrysalis that only in the past few centuries have people even suspected there was a connection between the bright creatures and caterpillars.

• Hardiness. Butterflies can be found within a few hundred kilometres of the North Pole and on mountains far above the treeline. They are most prolific and diverse in the tropics. (The only place devoid of the creatures is Antarctica.) There are several thousand species.

• Seasons. In temperate climates, butterflies are most common from early spring to fall and, in calm weather with sunshine, they are most active between 10 A.M. and 3 P.M. (Their relatives, the moths, are mostly nocturnal and at least ten times more numerous and diverse than diurnal butterflies.) The insects' adult life spans can vary from a few weeks to many months; in the Arctic, their complete life cycle may last several years because the larvae hibernate.

• Size. Queen Alexandra's Birdwing of Papua New Guinea is probably the world's largest butterfly, with a wingspan of almost 30 centimetres. (Some tropic butterflies may tag along after migrating species. In 1954, tropical butterflies as big as bats invaded Bologna, Italy. In 1934, a Toronto man found a bright specimen, with a wingspread of seven inches, on St. Clair Avenue West.)

• Behaviour. Some butterflies can learn. Several species patrol regular territories, defending their turf against other butterflies and even lunging at birds. Some species eat carrion. Butterfly fans can identify a species at a distance by its flight patterns (one Mexican species of white morpho has been described as a "flying pillowcase"). If they feast on fermented food, butterflies can get intoxicated and are easier to catch.

• Butterflies and people. Approached carefully, some butterflies can be coaxed to perch on sweaty fingers.

• Monarchs. These butterflies can cruise at about 16 kilometres an hour with bursts of speed up to 48 kilometres an hour, say researchers. Although the gaudy insects are known to be distasteful to birds, in 1957 several scientists at the University of Toronto reported that a Monarch tastes like dried toast and even "rather sweet." (Sources: *Handbook for Butterfly Watchers*, *The Butterfly Book*, *Collier's Encyclopedia*, *Globe* files.)

On your bikes

The modern bicycle, a feature of spring, was invented in April 1839. Some facts:

• Kirkpatrick Macmillan, a young Scottish blacksmith, invented the first bicycle that could be propelled without the rider's feet touching the ground.

• In June 1842, Mr. Macmillan (nicknamed "Daft Pate" because of his interest in bikes) rode his machine from Dumfries to Glasgow. The 64-kilometre journey took two days – a good time, say historians, in view of the condition of the roads and the technology. On the way, he was fined five shillings for narrowly missing a small child.

• In 1845, fellow Scot Gavin Dalzell improved Mr. Macmillan's bike: He moved the pedals under the saddle, from under the handlebars.

He who hopes

On April 14, 1917, Lazarus Ludovic Zamenhof died. He was also known as Dr. Esperanto ("he who hopes"), the inventor of a "universal tongue" designed to unite humanity. Some notes:

• Universal languages have been devised for centuries. Between 1880 and 1907, 53 were proposed. The number has continued to grow – up to 1,000 by some estimates. They include Logopandecteision (all its words have seven syllables) and Solresol (a 12,000-word language that uses only the do-re-mi of the musical scale).

• Volapuk, or "world speak," is based mainly on English but is mostly German in structure; one of its verbs has 505,440 different forms. After a few years' incubation in Germany, it spread to France. In 1889, Volapuk peaked in popularity, with an estimated one million speakers worldwide and a convention in Paris where even the waiters spoke the language. Then its inventor, J. M. Schleyer, argued with followers over grammar.

• Concocted in 1887, Esperanto is one of the most successful artificial tongues. Currently, there may be as many as 15 million speakers. The language was designed by Dr. Zamenhof to help create a brotherhood of mankind. Adolf Hitler executed thousands of Esperantists and Joseph Stalin put 11,000 into labour camps. On the other hand, Albania once seriously considered making Esperanto a mandatory language. Some Japanese find Esperanto easier to learn than European languages.

• Ido was developed by a breakaway group of Esperantists.

• Idiom Neutral is a language created by ex-Volapukists and disgruntled Esperantists.

Faithful service . . .

From a tombstone in Woolwich, south London: "Sacred to the memory of Major James Brush, killed by the discharge of a pistol by his orderly 14 April 1831. Well done good and faithful servant."

. . . Difficult return

On April 16, 1912, the *Titanic* converged with an iceberg. The luxury liner was carrying a squash court for the exercise of its rich passengers; at four kilometres below the surface of the Atlantic, this is now the lowest of 37,000 squash courts in the world.

When luck strikes

• In April 1991, Emmet and Bernice Decoursey of Morell, Prince Edward Island, won their second $100,000 from the Lotto 6/49. The previous win was almost exactly 14 years earlier. Mrs. Decoursey attributed the disappearance of her husband's bouts of multiple sclerosis to the joy of winning the first $100,000. The odds against winning this lottery are said to be greater than being struck by lightning, reported the Canadian Press. A few years before the second jackpot, the Decoursey house was struck by lightning.

• Later in 1991, Kathleen Motzny waited seven weeks to claim $12.3 million in the Illinois lottery. Asked why she waited so long, she said it had been difficult to get time off work.

• In 1987, Sheelah Ryan set a North American record by claiming the jackpot in the Florida lottery. "This is the first time I've ever won $55 million," said the 63-year-old mobile-home resident.

LSD trip

On April 16, 1943, Swiss chemist Albert Hoffmann accidentally manufactured and consumed LSD-25 while working in his laboratory. Thinking he was ill, he went home, thus going on the first LSD trip.

Thumb-sucking

Self-indulgent behaviour is sometimes called "thumb-sucking" – for instance, when an author just writes to please himself. Here's a thumb-sucker on thumb-sucking:

• Thumb-sucking begins in the womb.

• One-third to one-half of children between the ages of three and five suck their thumbs. Observers say the habit is more common among passive, shy youngsters. Based on a study of children between 1952 and 1971, Dr. Frank Popovich, a University of Toronto dental researcher, said children from large families, the offspring of executives and professionals, and those with longer weaning periods were more likely to suck.

• Dentists still take a dim view of the habit, although they now say that thumb-sucking is a problem only if continued after the permanent teeth sprout. Psychologists argue that banning the thumb doesn't work and underlying stress should be examined.

• Thumb-sucking may continue for years. Anthi Tsamtsouris, a professor of pediatric dentistry at Tufts University in Medford, Massachusetts, told the *Boston Globe*'s Madeline Drexler that in the several years since the *Wall Street Journal* wrote about thumb-sucking professionals, she had spotted four well-dressed adults driving to work with their thumbs in their mouths.

Marathons

The Boston Marathon is held on the third Monday of April. First run in 1897, it is among the most famous of world marathon races – and the first to admit women to competition (1972). Some notes:

• How long is a marathon? It depends. In 490 BC, a Greek soldier supposedly ran from Marathon to Athens, about 40 kilometres. In 1896, when the modern Olympics were revived, 26 miles (41,843 metres) was the distance. In 1908, at the British Olympics, an extra 385 yards (352 metres) was added so the race could begin at Windsor Castle and end in front of the royal box at the London stadium. In 1924, this 42,195 metres was standardized. Because of differing terrains, records for the world's marathons are not officially recognized.

• How many marathons can a person run? *The Guinness Book of Records* says that Thian Mah (1926-88) of Canada ran 524 marathons from 1967 until his death. Three marathons have been run in three consecutive days by a Scotsman.

• Who can run a marathon? In 1976, a 98-year-old Greek ran the Athens Marathon – but he took seven hours, 33 minutes. Mothers say that compared with childbirth, running a marathon is child's play.

Significant digits

• Two: Macabre 18th-century tales about exhumed corpses found to have clawed the interior of their caskets were not entirely fanciful, writes Jim Holt in the *Republic*. "Graveyard excavations reveal that nearly 2 per cent of those interred before the advent of embalming in the 20th century were buried alive."

• Eight: The average Caucasian sprouts eight metres of beard during his lifetime. Norwegian American Hans Langseth is credited with the record, a 5.33-metre beard. The longest deadly beard may have been the 2.7-metre growth of Hans Steiniger; in 1567, the Austrian burgomeister tripped over it, fell downstairs, and died.

• 17.3: Morning sickness in pregnant women lasts an average of 17.3 weeks, stretching to a full nine months for 10 to 20 per cent of women. Anywhere from 50 to 90 per cent of pregnant women have some symptoms.

• 46: A survey of 1,255 adults by New York's American Museum of Natural History has found that 46 per cent don't believe humans evolved from earlier species.

• 75: Top-quality ketchup would take at least 75 years to flow across Canada.

• 80: Almost 80 per cent of people, especially the creative and imaginative, will experience a nighttime tremor called "sleepy lurch." It occurs at the point of drowsiness/falling asleep and can even jerk a person out of bed.

• 3,000: When North American gardeners battle dandelions, crabgrass, clover, and chickweed, they are tackling European imports. There are 3,000 plant species from other parts of the world growing in North America.

Getting the bird

Spring means an increase in birdsong. Bird enthusiasts can often identify a species by its call alone. A sampling of the range of their chatter, as transcribed in the *Peterson Field Guides* to eastern and western birds:

Woo-ho, woo-woo, woo-ho (tundra swan).

Yeeb (male mallard).

Frahnk, frahnk, frahnk (great blue heron).

Ker-loo! Ker-loo! (whooping crane).

Ow-ooo-ur (male eider).

Kor-r-r (female eider).

Ow-owdle ow (old squaw).

Hoo-hoot (flammulated owl).

Vrrrip (Allen's hummingbird).

Caw, caw (American crow).

Chip, chupety swee-ditchety (Canada warbler).

Oh-dear-me (golden-crowned sparrow).

Hey Al (razorbill).

Tory-tory-tory-tory (Kentucky warbler).

Who was the Bard?

 On April 26, 1564, William Shakespeare was baptized. His birthday is celebrated on April 23, based on a fairly safe conjecture that three days elapsed before he was taken to the font. So little is known for certain about the Bard's life that a few people doubt that this son of a glover wrote his own plays. Some of the 58 pretenders to Shakespeare's title:

• Sir Francis Bacon. Delia Bacon of Boston wrote a book in 1857 suggesting that this philosopher-politician, her ancestor, wrote the plays. Soon after, she was confined to a mental institution.

• The Earl of Oxford, Edward de Vere. In 1921, T. J. Looney argued that this nobleman stopped writing his own poems and started writing Shakespeare's plays. The earl died in 1604, the plays continued appearing until 1611; Oxfordians say that a syndicate carried on.

• Christopher Marlowe. This dramatist was killed in a drunken brawl in 1593. U.S. drama critic Calvin Hoffman said Marlowe's death was faked to avoid a charge of heresy; he continued to write, using Shakespeare as a stooge.

• A Persian. The Persian words sheikh and pir mean "venerable sage," reported theatre producer Peter Brook in 1990. A Tadjik in Russia once asked him if it wasn't obvious that Shakespeare came from the Middle East.

The tabloids say . . .

- Fed-up passengers push plane onto runway (*Weekly World News*).
- Satanists order pizza and eat delivery man (*Sun*).
- Michelle Pfeiffer: I hate being beautiful (*News Extra*).
- Susan Sarandon: Getting older is a real turn on (*Weekly World News*).
- Couple remarry – 50 years after divorcing (*National Enquirer*).
- Teen's belch brings sister out of a coma (*Sun*).
- I mooned a werewolf . . . and he nearly killed me (*Weekly World News*).

Thought du month

"People who make budgets are nervous when there are problems in society. The basis of a restful budget is no problems in society." – Maharishi Mahesh Yogi, 1973, addressing the Illinois State Legislature.

May

May Days through the ages

May 1 is the traditional day for celebrating spring in Europe, a favourite peasant festival in many countries. It was a day of fertility rites (putting up maypoles, choosing May queens and kings) and folklore ("washing the face in the May Day morning dew will beautify the skin.") Some history:

• In old England, May Day was one of the most important festivals of the year. Church leaders did not like its pagan associations. The Puritans banned the holiday in 1644.

• In 1889, the International Socialist Congress, meeting in Paris, chose May 1 as Labour Day. It soon was associated with the far left.

• In the early 19th century, May Day belonged to London chimney sweeps. In this century, it has been Quebec's day for moving house and beginning new leases.

• The international distress call, May Day, is based on the French *M'aidez* ("help me").

You've got rhythms

U.S. scientists have discovered a gene that governs the sleeping and waking cycles in mammals. Notes about the biological clock:

• Throughout the day, more than 100 internal functions – including cell division, adrenal gland activity, DNA synthesis, temperature, and blood pressure – peak at various times.

• Most people can wake up for work in the morning without the use of an alarm clock, according to researchers at Duke University.

• Alertness peaks in late morning when body temperature is high and memory and problem-solving abilities are sharper than average. At noon, eyesight is best.

• Most normal births occur between midnight and 8 A.M.

• People sleep fewer hours than most mammals, but most mammals sleep more hours than other creatures. Some fish, insects, and plants don't sleep at all.

• Researchers say the link between lunar and monthly cycles is psychological rather than physical. (The Earth's pull on a human body is 5,012 times as strong as the moon's.) For instance, werewolves are probably fooling themselves.

Our pride is showing

• On May 9, 1880, George Brown, the first publisher of the *Globe* and a Father of Confederation, died from gangrene after being shot on March 25. The newspaper published his obituary, on page three, and the results of his autopsy. It was noted with pleasure that our late publisher's brain tipped the scales at 55 ounces, three drams – the largest brain his doctor had ever weighed.

• In 1791, the guillotine was invented. The first person to come under its blade was Duval Bertin, a distant relative of the *Globe*'s reporter Oliver Bertin.

Nonsense soundings

May 12 is the birthday of Edward Lear (1812-88). Like a lot of authors, he wrote nonsense. Some notes:

• As writers from S. J. Perelman to Monty Python's Graham Chapman have observed, words and phrases such as medical terms have their own rhythms. Absurd or meaningless words are sometimes valued for their own sake.

• The ancient Greeks referred to non-Hellenic persons as "barbarians," apparently imitating the nonsensical sounds foreigners made (*bar-bar-bar*). A similarly derived word is jargon (from an Old French word for the twittering of birds).

• Nonsense has links to the divine. Speaking in tongues, or glossolalia, is abnormal, inarticulate chatter under religious influence; it has been a feature of several religions. The oracle of Delphi, the celebrated and influential ancient Greek forecaster, was a middle-aged woman who chewed leaves, whiffed vapours, and then spoke – intelligibly or otherwise. Her nonsense was then translated into ambiguous verse by priests.

• Meaningless catchphrases have been popular through the centuries. In his *Extraordinary Popular Delusions* (1841), Charles Mackay writes that, many years earlier, there had been a craze in London among vulgar wits and mischievous urchins to shout "*Quoz!*" at innocent people in the street, thus creating mirth.

• In 1846, modern nonsensical verse made its début in Edward Lear's *The Book of Nonsense*. A decade earlier, Lear had created limericks to amuse children.

• Skilled literary nonsense is rare, notes the *Encyclopedia Britannica*. Top practitioners include mathematician Lewis Carroll ("Twas brillig and the slithy toves"), Catholic apologist Hilaire Belloc ("The fleas that tease in the high Pyrenees"), and former editorial writer Ogden Nash ("What would you do if you were up a dark alley with Caesar Borgia/ And he was coming torgia?").

• In 1892, English music-hall star Lottie Collins popularized the smash-hit song "Ta-ra-ra boom-de-ay." In this century, "scat" (improvised jazz singing) has contributed such phrases as "ooh-bop shebam." Novelty songs in the 1940s included such hits as "Hey! Ba-Ba-Re-Bop" (Tex Beneke & The Glenn Miller Orchestra) and "Mairzy Doats" (The Merry Macs).

• The current trend is to wordless lyrics, says arts writer Steven Rosen of the *Denver Post*, adding that examples from the past few decades include: "Rama Lama Ding Dong" (The Edsels), "Na Na Hey Hey" (Steam), "Da Doo Ron Ron" (Crystals), "De Do Do Do, De Da Da Da" (The Police), "Mmm Mmm Mmm Mmm" (Crash Test Dummies).

• Catchy, rhythmic nonsense can cross national boundaries. Since it began in 1956, the Eurovision Song Contest has included such titles as "Boum-Badaboum" (Monaco, 1967), "Boom-Bang-a-Bang" (Britain, 1969), "Boom Boom Boomerang" (Austria, 1977), and "Yamma Yamma" (Finland, 1992).

Significant digits

• Two: Two people have jumped off New York's Empire State Building at the 86th floor and been blown back into the 85th floor.

• Three: Chimpanzees hold the intercourse speed record for the animal kingdom – three seconds.

• Four: The average person takes approximately 18,000 steps a day, says author Russell Ash in *The Top 10 of Everything*. A lifetime's plodding amounts to almost four times around the Earth.

• 32: In more than 70 countries and territories of the world, writes Peter Kincaid, people drive on the left-hand side of the road. The Australian professor, author of *The Rule of the Road: An International Guide to History and Practice*, says this amounts to 32 per cent of the world's motorists.

• 100: "During the Middle Ages, scholars estimate, the average person saw no more than 100 people in his entire lifetime; fame was a rare commodity," writes William Ecenbarger in *Chicago Tribune* magazine.

Mother's Day thoughts

Mother's Day is the second Sunday in the month. Call her.

• "Women get depressed twice as often as men," writes Madeline Drexler in the *Boston Globe* magazine. "In nearly all Western cultures, and regardless of race, income level, education or occupation, this statistic holds true, says the American Psychological Association."

• Among macaque monkeys in Japan, mothers and offspring use the same cry to find each other, reports Steven Green, a biology professor at the University of Miami. He recalls a case,

25 years ago, of a mother macaque that wailed for hours for her baby – unaware it had died. Eventually, another female arrived from three hills away and hugged her. Markings showed she was the grandmother of the dead infant. "They hadn't seen each other for years," Dr. Green told the *Miami Herald*. "She was responding to her own daughter's call – one that says, more or less, 'I want my mommy.'"

Rough ballgame

Baseball seems to have become gentler over the years. On May 15, 1894, during the game's dirtiest decade, the Baltimore Orioles were playing the Boston Beaneaters. Boston's Tommy Tucker slid into third base and was kicked in the head by Hall-of-Famer John McGraw. Tucker arose and started punching it out with McGraw; the fans' enjoyment was marred when someone noticed the right-field bleachers were on fire.

Wonderful theories of Oz

May 15 is the birthday of L. Frank Baum (1856-1919), author of *The Wonderful Wizard of Oz*, the 1900 bestseller. This classic has been called badly written, has been banned by librarians, and, in recent years, has been termed an allegorical  work. Some theories, partly tongue-in-cheek, about Baum's simple tale:

• Political. Frank Baum was a Democrat prairie populist who endorsed William Jennings Bryan when he ran unsuccessfully for president in 1896 against William McKinley. Bryan's policy was to help the depressed farm sector with "bimetallism" –

minting silver as well as gold coins to create a more stable monetary system. A theory, elaborated in 1964, has it that Dorothy (average citizen) encounters the Scarecrow (the farmer), the Tin Man (the dehumanized, eastern industrial worker), and the Cowardly Lion (Mr. Bryan, who opposed the Spanish-American war). They travel to the Emerald City (Washington) on the Yellow Brick Road (the gold standard) after Dorothy loses her magical silver shoes (the silver standard; the 1939 MGM movie switched to ruby slippers to exploit colour). The populist movement is dissolved, Dorothy returns to Kansas.

• Economic. Dr. Hugh Rockoff of Rutgers points out in his economics classes: Oz is the abbreviation for ounces (of gold), the Wicked Witch of the East is eastern financiers (or pro-gold ex-president Grover Cleveland), the Witch of the West is malign nature (or William McKinley), and the wizard himself is perhaps Mark Hanna, the Republican Party chief, "considered for a time to be a sinister power behind the throne."

• Religious. Dorothy's adventure is a secular version of a religious account of creation, fall from grace, and return to paradise, says Dr. Paul Nathanson of the McGill Centre for Medicine, Ethics and Law.

• Feminist. Dorothy, a quintessentially feminine yet adventurous child, befriends a collection of pathetic and incompetent male characters while rapidly developing from an uninspired schoolgirl to someone who precipitates action. Together, they journey to the Emerald City to visit "the great, all-knowing patriarch," writes Justine Hankins in the *Guardian*. "Masculinity, however, proves to be ineffective and foolish."

Academy Awards

On May 16, 1929, the first Academy Awards ceremony was held. The dinner was attended by only 200 insiders from the movie industry and ignored by the press.

Queen Victoria

On May 24, 1819, the future Queen Victoria was born. By the time of her death in 1901 she ruled the British Empire – the biggest political organization in the history of the world, containing at its peak a quarter of the Earth's land surface and more than a quarter of the human race. Some notes:

• In 1837, when Victoria inherited the throne, the British monarchy was in sad shape. It was commonly assumed that the institution would not survive the march of democracy and the achievement of universal suffrage. In 1854, the Crown was so bitterly attacked by the press that Victoria threatened to abdicate, writes historian David Thomson.

• Victoria was not a Victorian. Her husband, the priggish Prince Albert, was responsible for setting the tone of strait-laced propriety and moral earnestness associated with her reign. Victoria had no racial prejudice, loathed bigotry, and ignored the fact that servants who waited on her table were often soused. She was openly anti-clerical and regarded herself as a Liberal.

• In the autumn of 1871, the Queen was sick and her son had caught a dangerous illness from the bad drains at Sandringham Palace – similar to the disease that had killed his father. When the Prince of Wales made a sudden recovery, Victoria – for the first time in her life – issued a personal letter of thanks to her people. The subsequent wave of public sympathy was heightened when an assassin tried to knock her off, two days after a service of thanksgiving. Republicanism was dead in England.

• The Queen owned 83 dogs and knew every one by name.

• The Queen's personal physician was Sir James Reid. When appointed in 1881, writes Richard Gordon in *The Alarming History of Medicine*, Victoria was fit but overweight and inclined to hypochondria; she summoned her doctor up to six times a day. In his 20 years of service, writes Dr. Gordon, Sir James never saw Victoria with any of her clothes off.

• Victoria was seldom "not amused." (That famous comment has not been conclusively linked to her and may have been a reaction to a bawdy joke.) In 1887, she slipped away to visit the circus secretly. In 1890, a visiting granddaughter wrote that the Queen had "laughed until she was red in the face." In 1896, a grandson was trying to teach her to lob a boomerang.

• Victoria Day has been a Canadian holiday since 1845 – and the Monday of a long weekend since 1952.

Victorian lit

• Women were thought to be much more susceptible emotionally and, thus, more vulnerable to books. Loran Sage, author of *The Woman Reader 1836-1914*, reports that Victorian women frequently complained it was hard to be left alone with a book. Some authors were forbidden, French novels were reviled, Shakespeare bowdlerized, and some girls were given schoolbooks with pages pasted together.

• When Charles Dickens killed off Little Nell in *The Old Curiosity Shop*, writes A. A. Gill in the *Sunday Times* of London, men were "drowned in a wave of grief" by what seems to modern readers a saccharine passage. (Victorian men cried openly, both for pity's sake and for sentimentality.) An Irish member of Parliament, Daniel O'Connell, read the Dickens novel on a train and burst into tears. "He should not have killed her," he groaned, and threw the book out the window.

A hard-boiled guy

May 27, 1894, was the birthday of Samuel Dashiell Hammett, an author who largely created the hard-boiled school of American detective fiction. Some notes about a man whose life paralleled his fiction:

• Hammett was a real-life private investigator; he dropped out of school at 13 and worked in a variety of jobs until he joined the Pinkerton detective agency. He enjoyed the independence and variety of being a "Pink." Although Hammett was a tall, thin man with reddish hair combed into a high pompadour, he could shadow suspects for days without being spotted.

• He took a leave of absence to serve as an army ambulance driver during the First World War (Sergeant Hammett never left the United States), and he contracted tuberculosis. This illness left him frail and unable to do much besides try his hand at writing. "Hammett," in the words of writer Nunnally Johnson, "had no expectation of being alive much beyond Thursday."

• He began with pulp-fiction short stories, and then between 1927 and 1932 he produced five novels. *The Maltese Falcon* (1930), considered to be his best work, introduces world-weary detective Sam Spade. *The Thin Man* (1932), later to spawn radio and movie series, contains a portrait of his companion, Lillian Hellman, as Nora Charles.

• Hammett "belonged to the vanishing species of the self-educated intellectual," wrote a *Globe* reviewer in 1975, "a loner who mixed effortlessly, a cynical romantic" who lied unhesitatingly about his tubercular 48-year-old body to enter the Second World War.

• *The Maltese Falcon* made Hammett a darling of literary society. He drank and spent heavily (his *Thin Man* was written while barricaded in a New York hotel, sober and desperate to earn some cash), and he worked as a Hollywood scriptwriter, making $100,000 a year in the depths of the Depression.

• After 1934, Hammett devoted his time to left-wing political activities and civil-libertarian causes. In 1951, during the Communist-hunting era, Hammett drew a six-month jail term for refusing to name some names that, in fact, he did not know.

• After 1934, Hammett's career as an author was essentially over, despite a few attempts at writing. Impoverished and burned out, he lived in his final years on the charity of others, and died of lung cancer in 1961.

Talking birds

In May 1994, kea parrots in New Zealand, keyed-up from high-calorie snacks given to them by tourists, were wrecking cars, tents, and boats. The sturdy kea nests in mountains high above the treeline, says *Collier's Encyclopedia*. In winter, it must forage for food and "it has become a sheep killer with a bounty on its head."

But parrots are better known for their brilliant talking than for senseless violence. There is a case of a parrot in Alaska, hired to do a TV commercial for the telephone company, that had his lines beak-synched; Alascom thought Pepper sounded too human and it hired a human who could sound more like a parrot. A few more words:

• The grey parrot of Africa is unsurpassed as a talker – the male may perfectly echo human speech. Two dozen species of Amazon parrots are also excellent mimics.

• Parrots often make it past 60 years and can outlive their owners, with whom they bond closely. Descriptions of their personalities range from "affectionate" to "cynical."

• Lost birds have been returned to owners because they could repeat their full names. In 1954, a Dutch couple in Toronto, who spoke little English, were able to return a budgie that told them: "My name is Tippy Brasseur and I live at 859 Davenport Rd., Lakeside 2277."

• Birds can imitate sounds other than speech. In 1952, Coco of Syosset, New York, was able to walk the lawns of her restaurant home unmolested – local cats were afraid of her barking. Polly II, a parrot living in Fleet Street's Cheshire Cheese pub during the Blitz, used to cause havoc when he mimicked the whistle of an incoming high-explosive bomb; somehow, he survived the war.

Everest: Tall stories

On May 29, 1953, the fact that two climbers had conquered the world's highest mountain was being kept secret. The news that Edmund Hillary and Tenzing Norgay had reached the summit was held for the Queen's coronation on June 2. Some Everest information:

• In 1841, a British geological team surveyed the mountain from 160 kilometres away. (It belongs to 200 or so Himalayan peaks that are unsurpassed in loftiness.) In 1852, a Bengali clerk checking the figures discovered it was the highest mountain in the world. The altitude worked out at exactly 29,000 feet (8,839 metres), but the surveyors reported it as 29,002 feet for credibility.

• The mountain, called Peak XV, was renamed in honour of Sir George Everest, India's pioneering surveyor-general. (The Tibetans call it Mount Chomolungma, which means either Mother Goddess of the World or Lady Cow, depending on how it is spelled and pronounced.)

• In 1924, George (Because-It's-There) Leigh-Mallory and Andrew Irvine were 200 yards from the peak when fog closed in and they disappeared forever from their team. A few mountaineers believe there is a camera somewhere on the mountain with film proving they made the summit.

• Europeans heard about abominable snowmen on Everest as early as 1921.

• Edmund Hillary, a New Zealand beekeeper, described the view from the top as "monotonous. Not spectacular." His colleague, Tenzing Norgay, who had tried six times previously to reach the peak, died in 1986 without revealing who stood on the summit first.

• Everest has since been climbed many times. Mr. Tenzing's son, Norbu Tenzing, has been part of an environmental group tackling debris left by climbers at "the highest trash pit in the world."

The tabloids say ...

• Lost baby crawls five miles to get home (*Weekly World News*).
• Plucky poodle saves teen from giant squid (*Sun*).
• Five-year-old whiz kid can build atom bomb (*Globe*).

• "Our child was conceived while freefalling," says proud mom (*Sun*).

• Hanging judge by day – rock singer by night (*National Examiner*).

• Killer vultures attack graduation ceremony (*Weekly World News*).

Thought du month

"If you can't spot the sucker in the game in the first ten minutes, then it must be you." – Poker saying.

June

Useless person?

On June 1, 1933, Lya Graf sat on J. P. Morgan's knee, in a Senate room in Washington. She was a midget, perched on the surprised banker by a quick-thinking circus flack while Mr. Morgan was waiting to testify about the stock-market crash. The photograph of their pose became world famous and the banker quickly capitalized on the smiling snapshot to "humanize" himself. Miss Graf, however, was a shy and sensitive woman who felt hounded by the resulting fame. Two years later, she returned to her native Germany. She was half-Jewish. In 1937, the Nazis arrested her as a "useless person" and shipped her to Auschwitz.

The love that won't go away

In early June 1992, an obsessed fan who pestered Olympic skating star Katarina Witt with threatening letters and nude photos of himself was sentenced to three years in a California mental hospital. Some notes on "erotomania," the love of an inappropriate or unobtainable person:

• This rare, obsessive love is found in people who are "a bit pathetic, not successful at sexual relationships," says British psychiatrist David Nias. It may be hard to recognize because, arguably, the greatest love affairs are obsessively frantic and jealous. (The first case was diagnosed by a French psychiatrist in 1921.)

• Not only celebrities are at risk, says Dr. Nias. Anyone perceived as a superior could become a victim. "Typically, women will fall in love with their bank managers because they were nice about their overdrafts."

• Dr. Jonathan Segal of Palo Alto, California, distinguishes between male and female erotic obsessives. Women believe their love is reciprocated; men know their feelings are not, but pursue their love objects anyway.

• California psychiatrist Park Dietz has studied 1,800 letters to public figures containing threatening and inappropriate messages. (For instance: "Please don't be afraid when God allows me to pull you out of your body to hold you tight.") He found that messages containing outright threats, obscenity, or sheer abusiveness were written by those least likely to try to see a celebrity in person.

• Erotic obsession can last a lifetime, and erotomaniacs are likely to become dangerous, writes Geraldine Bedell of London's *Sunday Times*. "If you become a target, the slightest twitch of the curtains will be interpreted by the person waiting outside as encouragement." (Sources: *Los Angeles Times, Observer, New York Times*.)

Lawn mowers: A few cuttings

People with lawns may find themselves mowing frequently these days: experts recommend trimming turf often enough that only a third of the blade length is removed at any one time, to avoid retarding lawn growth. Some history of the mechanical aid to cropping:
• Edwin Budding, a foreman at a Gloucester textile plant, developed the lawn mower in the 1820s.
• The early mowers were large and heavy: Gardeners in the 1860s experimented with horse-drawn models to manicure lawns, but hoof marks and manure detracted from the desired effect.
• In 1919, Edwin George, a U.S. army colonel, took the motor from his wife's washing machine to produce the first gasoline-powered lawn mower. It helped create the middle-class vogue for manicured lawns.

The wave wasn't a giveaway?

In June 1993, a group of construction workers in Uruguay apologized to the president of Brazil for stoning his car during a government visit. They thought he was a local official.

For book lovers

June 4 is the anniversary of the death of Giovanni Casanova (1725-98), a librarian and famous lover. Some facts about libraries:

• The Sumerians, who invented writing about 5,000 years ago, didn't make comprehensive collections of their records until the last dynasty had fallen in 1931 BC. The establishment of the first library of consequence is attributed to Rameses II, an Egyptian pharaoh in the 13th-century BC. China's first emperor tried to destroy collections of records earlier than his reign, so history could be seen to begin with him.

• In the Dark Ages, Europe's monastic libraries were surprisingly small, with only a few dozen books each. A 12th-century abbot, Ingulf of Croyland, forbade lending books under penalty of excommunication.

• With free public libraries, late returns became a problem. The record for an overdue book is 288 years (Britain, 1667-1955).

Another book lover

In 1994, film star Kim Basinger told *USA Weekend* that she has a book fetish. "It's sick," she said, "but I love dictionaries." A voracious reader, Ms. Basinger gets through 50 or so children's books a year, the magazine adds.

Birth of the Donald

June 9 is the birthday of Donald Duck (1934-). The refreshingly cranky Disney character, a lifelong bachelor, is an international star. He holds an honorary degree from Yale (Doctorate of International Friendship, 1939), has appeared on world postage stamps (including San Marino's, in 1970), and boasts a German-based international appreciation society (founded in 1977) that campaigned for a Donald Duck chair at the University of Hamburg.

A uniform sight

In June 1952, the first residents began moving into Levittown on Long Island, New York. The housing division, built by William Levitt, is considered the first modern suburbia. (The word "suburb" has been in the English language since the 14th century.) Some notes:

• Mr. Levitt revolutionized the concept of building houses after the Second World War by providing affordable homes for returning veterans. He used poured-concrete slabs for foundations and prefabricated walls to create almost-identical dwellings. His 800-square-foot, two-bedroom Cape Cod cottage-style houses – each with a garden in back and a front lawn – could be assembled at the rate of 36 a day. They rented for $60 (U.S.) a month, with an option to buy at $6,990. (His original houses now sell for more than $100,000.) The first family to buy a mass-produced house, Theodore and Patricia Bladykas, had twin daughters.

• "William Levitt was to suburbs (what) Henry Ford was to the auto," says Kenneth Jackson, author of *Crabgrass Frontier*, a history of U.S. suburbanization. The builder made the suburban, detached house a normal expectation for the middle class.

• The first Levittown sprang up in a potato field. It was followed by Levittowns in Pennsylvania and New Jersey, as well as inspiring scores of tract developments around the continent in the 1950s and 1960s.

• The first town almost wasn't built. Republicans on the town council of Hempstead, New York, feared that a suburb filled overnight with young veterans and New Yorkers would change the local power structure forever. "What they didn't realize was that when you put young Democratic families into their own homes, they become Republicans," said Desmond Ryan, executive director of the Association for a Better Long Island.

Perjoratives

• Edsel: the name has become a synonym for failure; it's included in the 23rd edition of *Webster's Dictionary*. Up to 18,000 names for this car were tested on the U.S. public, including Henry, Zoom, Zip, and Drof. (Poet Marianne Moore contributed many suggestions, including Intelligent Bullet, Pastelogram, and Mongoose Civique.) A Ford executive rejected a shortlist that included Corsair, Citation, Pacer, and Ranger, opting for the original title: Edsel, although it had been derided in surveys and initially rejected by the Ford family.

• Tonto: the name of the Lone Ranger's friend and a word that means "stupid" in Spanish.

Significant digits

• Four: The right hands of right-handed people tend to be slightly larger than their left hands, says paleontologist Loren Babcock of Ohio State University. Some glove manufacturers make right gloves about 4 per cent larger than their mates.

• Six: "According to market research," writes Mike Hewitt in the *Independent*, "the average exercise bicycle has a life of no more than six weeks."

• Nine: Canada has 9 per cent of the world's renewable freshwater.

• Ten: After about ten days in hot weather, the body acclimatizes. It is able to sweat more efficiently, at a greater rate, and with less exertion. Active people can lose up to ten litres daily through breathing, sweating, and excreting. Water is the best all-round beverage to replace the lost fluids.

• Tennish: Telephoning people at 10 o'clock on Saturday night is probably a bad idea, according to author James Gilbaugh in *Men's Private Parts: An Owner's Manual.* His survey on sexual intercourse indicates that 10 P.M. Saturday is "happy hour."

• 24: In a 1994 survey of 500 women for *Redbook* magazine, pollsters found that 24 per cent would rather go to a dentist than shop for a bathing suit.

• 50: Fifty per cent of the U.S. baby-boom generation is college educated, reports the *Wall Street Journal.*

• 95: By one expert's estimate, about 95 per cent of people "experience music going through their head for some, and in some cases virtually all, of their waking lives," writes Steve Metcalf of the *Hartford Courant.* He cites the case of a wealthy U.S. woman with an advanced degree in English who awakens each morning to the sound of "It's Judy's Turn to Cry" by Lesley Gore.

• 200: In 1994, the closest living relative of Otzi – the 5,000-year-old Ice Man discovered in the Tyrolean Alps – that scientists were able to discover was 35-year-old Marie Mosely of Dorset Avenue, Bournemouth. Researchers have established that only 4 per cent of Europeans come from the same stock as the man preserved in a freezer at Innsbruck University; his 200-generation-old gene sequence does not occur outside Europe, and he seems to have no living relatives in the Tyrol.

• 210: Forty-year-olds should each plant 210 seedlings (or 70 trees that are ten years old) to mop up the carbon dioxide they generate in a lifetime, calculates the International Society for Arboriculture.

- 10,000: The sense of smell is at its peak in middle age, writes Diane Ackerman in *A Natural History of the Senses*. People in general can detect more than 10,000 different odours.
- One billion: The cost of treating gunshot wounds in the United States is about $1 billion (U.S.) annually. Also, most mammals die at the same age, contends management-science expert Theodore Modis in his book *Predictions*. Rabbits, dogs, cows, and elephants have all accumulated about one billion heartbeats when they expire.

Cultural landmark

June 12 is honoured among Canadians as the birthday of the "Social Studies" column in 1990 – it was part of a redesigned *Globe and Mail*. Its first item: "The most common cause of injury on the job: overexertion."

Potatoe hed wuz rite

On June 15, 1992, U.S. Vice-President Dan Quayle persuaded an elementary school pupil that "potato" needed a final "e." Some notes about spelling:
- English spelling appears to be a mess. For instance: "Though the rough cough and hiccough plough me through, I ought to cross the lough." However, computer analyses show 75 to 84 per cent of words are spelled according to a logical pattern. Unfortunately, the 400 or so irregular spellings are among the most frequently used words in English.
- Until Shakespeare's time, no one worried about "correct" spelling. Not even proper names were spelled consistently.

(All the surviving examples of the Bard's signature have different spellings.)

• There is no link between spelling and intelligence or literacy. Notable writers such as F. Scott Fitzgerald were very bad spellers, says *The Dictionary of Misinformation.* As much as 2 per cent of the population has no problem reading but has difficulty spelling; there are brain-injured adults who can read but not spell, and vice versa.

• Reformers have messed up spelling. "Island" acquired its "s" in the 17th century because of the mistaken belief the word came from the Latin insula. Similarly, "doubt" and "debt" picked up a silent "b."

• Early printers, many from the Netherlands, messed up English spelling. Also, until the late 16th century, lines of type were "justified" (stretched or compressed so all would be the same length) by abbreviating and contracting words or by adding extra letters (usually an "e") rather than extra space.

• Spelling can flip-flop. So-called British spellings of "-our" words such as "labour" – adopted at the *Globe and Mail* in 1990 – had been recommended by Sir John A. Macdonald in 1890, in a "minute of council." (Shakespeare used "center.") The *Globe* did not go along with Sir John at the time, and in 1949 was moved to defend its decision of more than half a century earlier to drop the "u" spellings, stating "whatever phonetic value the 'u' had in word endings has long since been lost."

• In 1973, an Ontario judge ordered a Preston teenager to write out seven misspelled words in a statement to police ten times. A human-rights group protested: "We believe that making a spelling mistake is not an offence in Ontario." (Sources: *The Cambridge Encyclopedia of Language, Globe* files.)

Bloomsday

June 16 is Bloomsday, when James Joyce enthusiasts around the world read and perform passages from his novel *Ulysses*:
• The novel is an account of a day in the city of Dublin, June 16, 1904. Its characters include Leopold Bloom, a Jewish, middle-aged advertising salesman and cuckold.
• Joyce, who nearly went blind while writing the 700-page book, intended it as a gift for Nora Barnacle, who ran away with him to the Continent at the age of 20 and finally married him in 1931. June 16 was the day of their first date.
• In 1922, the author presented the first published copy to Nora, who promptly offered to sell it to friend and art critic Arthur Power. Nora eventually read the classic "as far as page 27 counting the cover," according to the author.

Father's Day

The third Sunday in June. Some reasons for you to have tender feelings:
• Although there's no evidence for "male menopause," some sort of male climacteric seems to be experienced by about 50 per cent of men. Symptoms can include: withdrawal, irritability to the point of rage, conflict with authority figures, and decreased ability to concentrate. There are reports of business executives who forget their own names. These feelings are common for men between the ages of 40 and 45, according to Yale psychologist Daniel Levinson.
• Up to 90 per cent of expectant fathers report symptoms resembling the signs of pregnancy, according to a 1985 study by the University of Wisconsin-Milwaukee School of Nursing.

The syndrome is called "couvade" and can apply to many behaviours, ranging from energetic "nesting" activity, such as the addition of a new room, to dramatic physical changes, such as a distended abdomen. Atlanta obstetrician Cathy Bonk said expectant fathers with couvade symptoms should take the advice given to pregnant women: rest, take anti-emetic medicine and crackers, and drink tea.

• In his book *The First Men's Guide to Cleaning House* (St. Martin's), author E. Todd Williams writes, "A man I know, a leader in the drum movement, thinks of dusting as a trial of manhood. He runs a tape of Little Ricky and does his chest in rouge and cornmeal. With Babalu to soothe his soul, the house somehow gets clean enough."

• In 1992, police in Marana, Arizona, raided a gathering of six naked men who were drumming and chanting around a fire; authorities suspected satanic sacrifices. The men, who were questioned for two hours, were upset to learn that town attorney Kirk Cookson (a woman) had watched the interrogation from the shadows. "The woman was never identified," wrote Thoron Lane, a counsellor and president of the American Wellness and Wilderness Center. "She looked at our naked bodies. We were shamed as men." As well as Mr. Lane, those shamed included a retired businessman, two therapists, and two mental-health counsellors.

• Some books for men in 1993: *The Joy of Uncircumcising!* (Hourglass Book Publishing) by Dr. Jim Bigelow of Pacific Grove, California, and *When Men Are Pregnant: Needs and Concerns of Expectant Fathers* (Delta) by Jerrold Lee Shapiro, a clinical psychologist in Santa Clara, California.

• In 1994, the foreskin movement was the latest U.S. sexual/ human-rights cause, reported the *Philadelphia Inquirer*. "The movement even has its own martyrs, who are undergoing hypnosis and primal therapy to re-experience the pain. . . . They also are buying thousands of copies of *The Joy of Uncircumcising"* and regrowing their foreskins with the help of adhesive tape and weights. (A cry of pain, recorded in an interview: "I was circumcised . . . 70 years ago. I still feel rage.")

Playing our song

On June 24, 1880, "O Canada" was first performed. Written by Calixa Lavallee (1842-91), the lyrics at the time were only in French. Other anthem notes:
• Claude-Joseph Rouget de Lisle composed the world's first "popular" national anthem, "The Marseillaise." The French army engineer wrote the words and music one night in 1792 during a party, as France was preparing to fight Austria. Later, revolutionary mobs picked the song up and gave it its present name.
• The words of the Japanese national song date from the 9th century. The Dutch anthem has been sung since 1626.
• There are 11 anthems without words. The songs of Japan, Jordan, and San Marino have only four lines apiece.
• The tune to "God Save the King (Queen)" has been used at times by 20 nations, including Germany and Switzerland.
• In 1990, British clerics wanted to change the third verse of "God Save the Queen," which hopes the nation's enemies will be confounded and frustrated. When printed in 1745, the song had a fourth verse, about crushing the Scots; this was subsequently dropped as unlikely to promote national unity.
• In 1960, when Royal Navy musicians were updating the British Admiralty's anthem lists, they checked out the music for the Sultanate of Muscat and Oman. A local diplomat discovered the anthem hadn't been played since 1937, no one

could read the score, and most people in the sultanate regarded playing music as sinful. However, an old gramophone record seemed to match the sheet music. (Sources: news services, various encyclopedias.)

Keep watching the skies

 On June 24, 1947, Kenneth Arnold, an amateur pilot flying near Mount Rainier in Washington, saw a formation of nine discs. He said they were travelling at 1,900 kilometres an hour. The term "flying saucer" was coined by an anonymous copy editor who wrote the headline for Mr. Arnold's report.

• The next few sightings were confined to the U.S. Pacific Northwest. But, in three weeks, saucer reports were made in 40 states and six provinces.

• Some people saw flying discs, flying Yo-Yos, or "flying wash-tubs." Three men at Lake Deschenes in the Ottawa Valley saw a "flying stovepipe." Estimates of the objects' size ranged from 0.6 to 90 metres in diameter.

• At first, foreigners scoffed at the North American craze. Then reports came from other continents. On July 14, 1947, Chinese observers said, a saucer had landed at Shanghai but had disappeared on the black market.

Still keep watching

Over a 50-year period, a North American faces these risks of death:

From botulism: one in two million.

From fireworks: one in one million.

From tornadoes: one in 50,000.

From an airplane crash: one in 20,000.

From a giant asteroid hitting the Earth: one in 6,000.
(Source: *New York Times*.)

The tabloids say ...

- Vampire sues airline over busted coffin (*Weekly World News*).
- UFO aliens mugged in Manhattan (*Sun*).
- One in three blonde women aren't (*National Enquirer*).
- Man dumps wife to wed mother-in-law (*News Extra*).
- Doctors are mystified by girl who eats money; she prefers fives, says her mom, but will eat ones if she's really hungry (*Sun*).
- Milk hangovers are the worst (*National Examiner*).
- 85-year-old sky diver jumps from plane – and forgets to open his chute (*Weekly World News*).

Thought du month

"Kill all the rich people. Break up their cars and apartments. Bring the revolution home, kill your parents, that's where it's really at." – The credo, issued in June 1968, by young Greenwich Village revolutionaries calling themselves the Weathermen. They later changed their name to the Weather People, to avoid being sexist.

July

Canada Day

On July 1, 1867, the Dominion of Canada came into existence and John A. Macdonald was sworn in as the first prime minister. The British North America Act granted Canada independence from Britain, but the dominion was not allowed to deal directly with other states, control immigration, or command its own armed forces.

Mysterious Canadians

How others have seen us:
• In 1993, to give a rosy ending to his BBC television series "Lady Chatterley's Lover," the producer reunited the aristocrat and her gardener on an ocean liner bound for Canada. Some fans were baffled, reported the *Daily Telegraph*. Joan

McCluskie, secretary of the D. H. Lawrence Society, said, "It doesn't seem to be a better ending than the original. Perhaps it's designed to please Canadians."

• "Shakespeare is a drunken savage with some imagination whose plays can please only in London and Canada," said Voltaire.

Medical watch

• "Our bodies were designed to hunt by day, sleep at night, and never travel more than a few dozen miles from sunrise to sunset," writes Martin Moore-Ede in *The Twenty-Four Hour Society*. "Now we work and play at all hours, whisk off by jet to the far side of the globe, make life-or-death decisions, or place orders on foreign stock exchanges in the wee hours of the morning."

• Handwriting changes may be an early indication of Alzheimer's disease, according to Jean Niels, a researcher at the University of Cincinnati, who found that patients: often confuse words that sound alike, such as "nun" and "none"; have trouble with words containing silent letters (such as "through") or unusual combinations ("fright") and tend to spell these words the way they sound.

Mosquito bites

"Why me?" asked an irritated *Globe* editor, not known for her tendency to scratch, but a favourite nonetheless of mosquitoes. Some notes about one of the pests of summer:

• "Mosquito" is Spanish for gnat and originally applied to many small species of bloodsuckers.

• Worldwide, there are about 3,400 species of mosquitoes.

Canada has at least 77 species. The tropics have the most varieties, but the farther north you go, the greater the number of individual skeeters. Northern mosquitoes buzz louder, land harder, and itch more.

- Canadian researchers in the Arctic have reported a rate of 9,000 bites a minute. That would drain a person's blood in two hours.
- It is the females who bite, to get sustenance for their eggs. Male mosquitoes feed entirely on plant juices. Activity peaks at dawn and dusk. It takes 90 seconds for a biter to become fully gorged. A well-fed female can fly carrying twice her normal weight in blood.
- Hungry mosquitoes will attack a warm billiard ball, but they prefer people. They are attracted by carbon dioxide, lactic acid, moisture, and warmth; nervous, fidgety people are twice as likely to be bitten as calm individuals. Mosquitoes are twice as attracted to blue as to any other colour, and have a yen for people who eat bananas. Accumulated sweat is also a turn-on.
- Some species prefer to attack birds or reptiles. Charles Hogue, an entomologist at the University of Southern California, has said that only 10 per cent of the world's species are interested in biting humans and far less than that carry diseases.
- A mosquito bite begins to itch after about three minutes. This allergic reaction can diminish over the spring and summer as a person develops a tolerance; the bumps will be smaller and won't hurt as much. However, moving to a new region and being bitten by a different species means building a tolerance all over again.

Yankee Doodle Dandy

The Fourth of July is the closest thing Americans have to Canada Day. Some U.S. notes:

• The nickname for an American, especially one from New England, is "Yankee." The origin of the word, which seems to have arisen as a term of abuse, is unknown, but a plausible conjecture, says the *Encyclopedia Britannica*, is that the word comes from Jan Kees, the diminutive of Jan Cornelius, the Dutch version of John Doe.

• The U.S. Declaration of Independence was published on July 4, 1776. Only John Hancock, president of the continental congress, and Charles Thomson, secretary, signed it that day. Most founding fathers autographed it on August 2. One didn't get around to signing until 1781.

• Almost as many Americans fought for Britain as against Britain. John Adams estimated that one-third of people favoured rebellion, one-third opposed it, and the rest were indifferent.

• The "Minutemen" weren't volunteer farmers. Many were paid to serve, often by a farmer who wanted a stand-in to do his fighting for him.

• There's no evidence Betsy Ross created the first American flag. In 1780, a "Francis Hopkinson" sent the Board of Admiralty a bill for the design.

• The song "Yankee Doodle Dandy" was written by a British soldier to mock colonial bumpkins (the Yankee stuck a feather in his cap and called it "macaroni" or "fashionably Italian"). The unsophisticated Yankees didn't get it; they parroted the song, unaware of the insult.

Rah-rah rules

Some of the advice to cheerleaders, said the *New York Times* in 1990, taught at four-day summer camps in the United States that were devoted to the activity: Don't chew gum. No winking at your boyfriend. When an opposing player is hurt on the field, don't say, 'Okay, we got him good.'"

Significant digits

• Zero: The lifetime achievement of the Three Stooges includes more than 200 films between 1930 and 1965, one Academy Award nomination, and zero appreciation by the French.

• Half: In 1990, a study by Health and Welfare Canada found that about half of Canadians had been insulted or humiliated by someone who had been drinking.

• Five: "There are only five kinds of insects that are widely eaten," says Jan Crafford of the South African Entomological Society. "The others might not actually be toxic, but they taste awful."

• 200 to 300: There were only about 200 to 300 gunslingers of the Wyatt Earp type in the Wild West, estimates *The Oxford History of the American West*, adding that they tended to be Republicans.

• 400: The trend on Earth is towards longer and fewer days, says the *Guardian*. Growth rings on fossil corals indicate there were once 400 days in a year.

• Half a billion: There will be almost half a billion teenagers worldwide in the year 2010, says the *Sunday Times* of London; they will constitute the planet's largest consumer group.

No naughty bits

July 11 is the birthday of famous expurgator Thomas Bowdler (1754-1825). A few cutting remarks:

• In 1818, the first edition of *Bowdler's Family Shakespeare* appeared, including sanitized versions of four tragedies. "Nothing is added to the original text," says its title page, "but those words and expressions are omitted which cannot with propriety be read aloud in a family."

• The anonymous edition was actually the work of Harriet Bowdler, sister of Thomas. Thomas got the credit because, at the time, it was considered unseemly for a woman's name to appear in print.

• Thomas, a medical student, actually did some of the later editing on the ten-volume bowdlerized version of the Bard, and went on to clean up Edward Gibbon's *Decline and Fall of the Roman Empire* and produce a version of the Old Testament fit for children.

• For 11 years, the bowdlerized Shakespeare went unnoticed, but subsequently became popular in the Victorian era, going through 30 printings and turning into a staple of every genteel library. Until the turn of the century, many middle-class women never read the real Shakespeare and no child ever did.

• Some bowdlerizations: In *Romeo and Juliet*, Juliet's age is changed to 17 and her keenness to lose her virginity disappears; Hamlet's disgust over his mother's remarriage vanishes, eliminating most of the motive for his erratic behaviour; Macbeth's taunt "The devil damn thee black, thou cream-faced loon! Where got'st thou that goose look?" is softened to "Now friend, what means thy change of countenance?"

Is it dinosaur?

Dinosaurs thrived for roughly 130 million years. However, when their fossils pop up, they erode to dust in a few decades unless they are discovered and preserved; some dinosaurs are known only by a few discarded teeth. If unsure about fragments of material, paleontologists can lick them. Fossils will stick to the tongue. Rocks will not.

Leprosy today

July 11 is the birthday of Robert the Bruce (1274-1329). The Scottish king died of leprosy. Some facts about what was once the "unclean" scourge and is now the least contagious of infectious diseases:

• Biblical leprosy was a collection of skin diseases and was regarded as a sign of sinfulness. (Syphilis was considered a form of leprosy.)

• Modern leprosy, or Hansen's disease, comes in two forms (nerve or skin type), can take many years to show symptoms, and works partly by suppressing the immune system. Scientists aren't sure how it spreads – but casual contact with victims is not enough. The bacilli attack the cooler parts of the body first, deadening nerve endings.

• Nowadays, most people outside the 30th parallels of latitude seem to be naturally immune to the disease. Their protection may be related to living standards; Europe once had 18,000 leprosy colonies, and studies of Scandinavian skeletons show that it was widespread in that region 1,000 years ago. Canada had two leprosy hospitals – by 1967, both were closed for lack of patients.

• Drugs developed during the Second World War can stop the progress of leprosy.

My kingdom for a theatre

On the evening of July 13, 1953, Alec Guinness dangled his leg over the balcony of a stage in Southwestern Ontario and intoned, "Now is the winter of our discontent made glorious summer . . ." The actor, as Richard III, was kicking off the first play of the first Stratford Festival.

Thunderstorms

• At this moment, there are an estimated 18,000 thunderstorms going on in the world, and 100 bolts strike the earth each second.

• Slightly more than half of all lightning-caused deaths in the United States occur indoors – the home is the No. 1 place to die from a thunderbolt. Also, almost one-third of all victims were killed because they sheltered under a tree.

• Animals can be victims. In 1989, two South African rhinoceroses under a tree were struck as they mated. When the pair regained consciousness, they reportedly looked at each other and abruptly took off in opposite directions.

• About 70 to 80 per cent of people will recover from a hit. As long as the lightning does not pass across the heart or spinal column, recovery is probable.

• Roy C. Sullivan, a Virginia forest ranger, holds the record for being struck by lightning. Between 1942 and 1977, he was zapped seven times. (Mr. Sullivan killed himself in 1983, apparently unlucky in love.)

Allons citoyens ...

On July 14, 1789, a Parisian mob stormed the Bastille, inspired by an erroneous newspaper report that 30,000 royal troops elsewhere in the city were slaughtering citizens. Some facts:
• The Bastille was a royal prison, the least important to break open in any fight against persecution because only people of unusual status were held there. (Alumni included Voltaire and the Man in the Iron Mask.)
• There were only seven prisoners being held when the fortress was stormed; two were lunatics and one was a man who, 30 years earlier, had been an accomplice to the attempted murder of Louis XIV with a penknife.
• The Marquis de Sade was almost freed in the storming; he had been moved out of his cell shortly before the assault.
• The mob was made up mostly of provincials. A formal list of the 633 citizens who were besiegers of the Bastille – a title of great honour in years to come – shows that only 200 were Parisians.

The birth of the blue

At this time of year, the weather in Canada can be damned hot – which is easier to write than it once was. In fact, profanity is so prevalent in society, according to the *Wall Street Journal*, that language once confined to barracks and barrooms is being heard in kindergarten classes. Notes on profanity, from *Globe* files and elsewhere:
• Sex, excretion, and the supernatural are the main sources of swear-words, according to the *Cambridge Encyclopedia of Language*.

• "Primitive man could swear before he could talk," wrote Burges Johnson in *The Lost Art of Profanity* (1948). ("Swearing" comes from the Old English swerian "to speak aloud.")

• Ancient swearing: The Greek philosopher Pythagoras would curse "by the number 4." The French poet Charles (Flowers of Evil) Baudelaire swore "by the sacred Saint Onion." In the 15th century, a Spanish monk led a campaign to curb widespread profanity among the clergy; his movement became the Holy Name Society.

• In 1532, author Francois Rabelais wrote *Gargantua and Pantagruel*; their swearing performances, it is said, have never been exceeded. A sample (translated) chapter begins: "Odsbodkins. What a devil. With a pox to them. I vow and swear by the handle of my paper lantern" and on and on.

• In 17th-century England, the Puritans established a system of fines for cursing; for instance, a duke paid 30 shillings on a first offence, a commoner was nicked for three shillings fourpence. Swearing included "as God is my witness" and "upon my life."

• Some languages, such as Arabic and Turkish, are famous for their cursing. Examples: "You father of 60 dogs" and "You ride a female camel."

• In 1944, 100 longshoremen in Port Arthur, Ontario, (now part of Thunder Bay) went on strike because a foreman had been swearing at them.

• In 1957, a Quebec provincial secretary suggested substitute swear-words for foul-mouthed habitants; they included *sapristi* and *saperlipopette* (untranslatable), and *sirop d'erable* ("maple syrup").

• In 1961, a man in Oakville, Ontario, who swore at his

wife – in front of his children – received two days in jail for contributing to juvenile delinquency. (His conviction was overturned on appeal.)

• In 1969, a Vancouver youth got two months in jail for swearing at Prime Minister Pierre Trudeau at a peace rally.

• In 1971, Mr. Trudeau mouthed something in the House of Commons that he later claimed was "fuddle-duddle."

Beginning the ascent . . .

All present-day organisms may have originated from sludge at the bottom of the ocean, according to NASA researchers in California. They contend that, in the first billion years of the Earth's history, it was bombarded by chunks of rock the size of Britain, creating continent-sized fireballs and vaporizing the top 300 metres of the oceans. "All life as we know it, including humans, may therefore be descended from primitive organisms that were protected from destruction by several (kilometres) of ocean water above them."

. . . Making a landing

On July 21, 1969, humans set foot on the moon; eventually a dozen astronauts would walk on its surface. Some quotes from a quarter-century ago:

• "At takeoff . . . the biggest engine in history burned as much oxygen as half a billion people, squandering 15 tons of fuel a second, riding an 800-foot spike of flame. The roar seemed to turn your entire body into one resonating ear. It was a proper instrument for writing our signature on the heavens, big enough to be read by God," said U.S. physicist/science-fiction writer Gregory Benford about *Apollo 11*.

• "Roughly 35 per cent of the people now living were not yet born when we went to the moon the first time, so in that sense, it's damn near ancient history," says former astronaut Edgar Mitchell. In 1971, he became the sixth man to walk on the lunar surface.

The first detective

July 24 is the birthday of Francois-Eugene Vidocq. When Edgar Allen Poe wrote the first detective story, *The Murders in the Rue Morgue* (1841), the creator of sleuth C. Auguste Dupin is thought to have been influenced by the memoirs of Vidocq (1775-1857), who established the world's first detective bureau in 1832 in Paris:

• Mr. Vidocq was an army officer, thief, and jailbreaker who approached the French authorities in 1809 with an offer to use his knowledge of the criminal world to catch crooks. Going straight, he experimented with fingerprinting, blood and ballistics tests, was an expert at disguise, and was among the first to keep detailed files on criminals. Using crooks to catch crooks, he was remarkably successful in tracking down offenders. He became chief of the criminal police in 1810, when he founded the Sûreté.

• After he retired, Mr. Vidocq lost his money, allegedly organized a daring theft to be reinstated as a cop, was dismissed, and became a private detective – but his firm was suppressed. His several volumes of memoirs, which inspired novelists such as Victor Hugo and Honore de Balzac, were exaggerated and were likely written by someone else.

• In 1990, a group of U.S. homicide detectives, prosecutors and defence attorneys, FBI and customs agents, and forensic-science experts formed the Vidocq Society, dedicated to solving murders long thought to be unsolvable. Membership is limited to 82, the number of years their namesake lived. Mr. Vidocq "was a sort of Everyman," said William Fleisher of Philadelphia, president of a society that was intended as a recreational club for sleuths. In 1992, although the society had no official standing, jurisdiction, or budget, it had helped crack a few cases, had been offered more unsolved murders than it could handle, and had plans for international expansion.

Who goes there?

• John Green of Harrison Hot Springs, British Columbia, a student of the legendary Bigfoot, has collected 1,000 "footprint events," says author David George Gordon in *Field Guide to the Sasquatch*. Some identification tips for travellers in the West Coast woods:
• A Sasquatch footprint looks like a human's, but would take a man's size 21 shoe. Some are as long (56 centimetres) as two human feet. The imprints are deep.
• Sasquatch have flat feet.
• Some footprints have a line of equal-sized toes, others have a bulbous "big" toe. Observers think the variation is partly explained by hoaxing.
• Bear prints are smaller, and if they show claw marks it's a dead giveaway the animal is not Bigfoot.

Vincent Van Gogh

July 29 is the anniversary of the death of painter Vincent Van Gogh (1853-90) from a self-inflicted gunshot. Since then, scientists and others have tried to explain the erratic behaviour and achievements – largely in his last four years – of the troubled genius. Some of the influences cited:

• Unconscious causes. He had a brother, the first Vincent Van Gogh, who died in infancy and his mother kept harping on the subject.

• Poisoning. Gauguin reports seeing Van Gogh trying to eat a tube of paint; this behaviour was also seen when Van Gogh was in an asylum. The Dutchman also kept an extremely untidy workplace and might have developed lead poisoning.

• Digitalis intoxication. This would account for Van Gogh's favouring the colour yellow and swirling halo effects. In two portraits of his last physician, Paul-Ferdinand Gachet, the painter includes a dark purple flower; purple foxglove is the source of digitalis. There is no evidence that Van Gogh took the drug – which can cause confusion, delirium, and a foggy yellow vision – but it was considered a panacea in the last century.

• Absinthe. The alcoholic beverage, now illegal in most countries, was a favourite with Van Gogh. This extract of wormwood leaves can produce exaltation, auditory and visual hallucinations, arousal, and blindness.

Van Gogh's charisma

• In 1990, the *Bangkok Post* contained this ad for a local nightspot: "Vincent Van Gogh Club. Happy hours 4 P.M. to 9 P.M. Beautiful atmosphere and great service."

• In 1995, 120-year-old Jeanne Calment of Arles, France, was the world's oldest human. She also had the world's longest memory. She disliked Vincent Van Gogh, says the *European*, even though he bought canvases from her husband's cloth shop: "He was an ugly man. He was strange and most people called him 'the nut' in Arles. And to think that his paintings are now worth millions!"

The tabloids say . . .

* Your pet may be plotting against you (*Weekly World News*).
* Dog lands plane after pilot has heart attack (*Sun*).
* Recession forces cheaters to seek cheaper affairs (*Star*).
* Clown kills his rival by making him laugh himself to death (*National Enquirer*).
    * It's the hottest new trend in medicine . . . drive-thru surgery (*Star*).
    * The amazing healing power of beer (*Sun*).
    * Woman commits suicide with Mexican food and baking soda (*Weekly World News*).

Thought du month

"Our ignorance of history makes us libel our own times. People have always been like this." – French novelist Gustave Flaubert.

August

The scourge of slavery

On August 1, 1834, slavery was abolished in British posses-
sions. It had been abolished formally in England in 1772 and
the British moved to stop the slave trade in 1807. A few notes:
• Canadian Indians practised slavery.
• Portuguese explorer Gaspar Corte-Real enslaved 50 Indian
men and women in 1500 in Newfoundland.
• The first slave transported directly from Africa to Canada
was sold in 1629 in New France. The French preferred Indian
slaves, English settlers preferred Africans. Slavery expanded
rapidly in Canada after 1783, when American Loyalists
brought their slaves with them.
• John Graves Simcoe, lieutenant-governor of Upper Canada,
tried to outlaw slavery in 1792. Opposition by landowners
meant he had to compromise: no additional slaves could be

imported into the colony and children of slaves were to be set free at the age of 25. Slavery began to decline; the last surviving former slave died in Cornwall, Ontario, in 1871.

• Because of its plantation economies, slavery was much more common in the United States. By the mid-1800s, the slave population had risen to more than four million.

• Before the abolition of slavery in the U.S. civil war, the Underground Railroad helped as many as 30,000 fugitive slaves to escape to Canada.

• Officially, no country has permitted people to be bought and sold since the 1970s.

Prejudicial language

• Racist: apparently entered the English language in 1936, as a borrowing from the French. The older term in English is "racialist."

• Sexist: an Americanism, has been traced to a lecture by Pauline M. Leet in 1965.

• Ageist: is the epithet used by kidnapped heiress Patricia Hearst in 1974 when her fiancé, Stephen Weed, said she was too young to know her own mind and make reasonable decisions – she had joined her abductors, the Symbionese Liberation Army.

• Speciesist: a term that appeared *circa* 1973 and is applied by animal-rights activists to those who believe that human beings are superior and animals can be killed, eaten, and used for scientific research.

• Languagist: at least a decade old, this word refers to one who believes some languages or dialects are superior to others.

A tower of babble

There are 5,000 to 10,000 languages and dialects in the world. Numbers are hard to pin down because opinions vary as to the definition of a language; also, for political or social reasons, people may not admit that they speak a certain language.

• Most complex tongues include: Chippewa (up to 6,000 verb forms) and Inuit (63 forms of the present tense and 252 inflections for simple nouns). In Chinese, one of the pronunciations of "i" has 84 meanings, including "dress," "hiccup," and "licentious."

• Number of words in the English language: 490,000 plus 300,000 technical terms. It is unlikely that any individual uses more than 60,000 and the average is probably 5,000 to 10,000.

Babbling Bruce

August 3 is the anniversary of the death of Lenny Bruce (1925-66), whom the *Encyclopedia Britannica* calls a "mordant nightclub comedian." His work was known for its blue language, improvisation, moralizing, and assaults on the audience's sensibilities. Persecuted and unemployed because of obscenity charges and drugs, Bruce died of a narcotics overdose on the day he learned that he was going to lose his house:

• Bruce's real name was Leonard Schneider. He was born in New York in 1925. His mother was a part-time comedian and his wife, Honey Harlow, was a stripper.

• Bruce had the knack of discovering an audience's taboos and breaking them. One evening in 1955, working as the emcee of a strip show, he walked on stage naked: "What's the big deal? This is what you came for, isn't it?"

• He began to perform in nightclubs. He attacked everything, including the American Civil Liberties Union. After a 1960 routine (*How to Relax Your Coloured Friends at Parties*), columnist Walter Winchell dubbed him "America's No. 1 Vomic."
• By 1961, Bruce had been imprisoned for obscenity. In 1964, in a New York trial, a city licensing official mimicked his routine for judges. The appalled comedian said, "This guy is bombing and I'm going to jail." In the final years, his New York conviction (overturned posthumously) as well as drug abuse, depression, and divorce took the edge off his humour.
• Bruce's admirers included lawyers, priests – and right-wing gossip columnist Dorothy Kilgallen, who appeared as a witness for him.
• After he died, the *Washington Post* stated in an editorial, "He was a social satirist, one of the boldest and one of the best."
• There was a broadway show, *Lenny*, after his death. The New York district attorney who had prosecuted him went backstage and congratulated the cast.

The magic bullet

On August 6, 1881, Alexander Fleming, discoverer of penicillin, was born. Penicillin and the antibiotics that followed in its wake are estimated to have added ten years to people's life expectancy.

Canada and the bomb

On August 6, 1945, at 8:15 A.M. Japanese time, the world's first nuclear war began. It lasted nine days, until Japan's surrender:
• Announcement of Hiroshima bombing by the Canadian Press: "Japan rocked today under the most devastating

August

destructive force ever known to man – the atomic bomb – and Canadian science and Canadian uranium played a large part in this epochal achievement."
• Local angle: "Canadian and British scientists, working in Montreal and here [in Washington] to harness the unprecedented power, the force of which in peace as well as war may alter the course of civilization." Anglo-American work began in North America a few weeks before Pearl Harbor.
• The next day, touching on fears about splitting atoms, a Toronto engineer said on CBC Radio, "There is no need to fear that the dropping of the atomic bomb on Japan is going to disrupt the force of gravitation, or destroy the entire universe under our feet."
• On August 9, when Nagasaki was bombed, U.S. president Harry Truman discussed the new technology: "The atomic bomb is too dangerous to be loose in a lawless world. That is why Great Britain, Canada, and the United States, who have the secret of its production, do not intend to reveal the secret until means have been found to control the bomb . . ." (Sources: *Globe* files, *Hiroshima* by John Hersey.)

Five parents

On August 7, 1993, Hannah Caylan Seeger was born in California. The infant has five parents. When John and Jo-Lynne Seeger of Huntington Beach wanted to adopt another child, they contacted the birth parents of their first adoptee, Nathaniel, for a second baby with the same traits. The biological parents – unmarried and living separately – declined to have another baby for the couple but they contributed their eggs and sperm, which were united in a laboratory. Because Jo-Lynne Seeger is unable to carry a child, Mr. Seeger's married daughter from a previous marriage volunteered to be the surrogate mother.

From the mouths of babes

Parents, says *The Book of You*, may expect these conversational milestones from their youngsters:
• Six weeks: coos.
• Four months: says "ah-goo." Makes razzing sound.
• Six months: babbles.
• Eight months: says "da-da" and "ma-ma" but not as names.
• Nine months: understands "no."
• Eleven months: says first word. Uses "da-da," "ma-ma" as names.
• Twelve months: says second word. Makes up gibberish sentences.

Eye of the dawn

August 7 is the birthday of Margaretha (Gerda) Zella Macleod (1876-1917), alias Mata Hari, alias German secret agent H-21. She was a dancer and self-mythologizing courtesan whose name has become synonymous for a seductive female spy:
• Gerda, raised in a Dutch convent and fond of military men, married in 1895 after she answered a joke lonely-hearts advertisement placed by the friends of Captain Rudolph Macleod. He was a Scottish-born womanizer in his 40s; the photo of the 19-year-old appealed to him.
• The couple had two children and went to Sumatra, where Rudy rejoined his Dutch regiment. He drank, chased women,

beat her, and treated her as a domestic slave, according to the book *Women Around the World and Through the Ages*. Her son died and her husband ran off at one point, taking their daughter. The couple returned to Europe and were divorced.

• Moving to Paris in 1905, she began a career as an exotic dancer from the East, calling herself Lady Macleod and then Mata Hari (Malay for "Eye of the Dawn"). Sometimes she was Indian, sometimes Javanese. The voluptuous stripper became the toast of many cities. By 1914, she was said to be the highest paid courtesan in Europe.

• During the war – she was trapped in Berlin at its outbreak and later shuttled to Paris, The Hague, and Madrid – she had many brief liaisons with military and government officials from several countries.

• The extent of Mata Hari's espionage, if any, is uncertain; she may have been a double agent. She was vague about dates and places and "was never to learn that if she could reinvent her past, so could others and use it against her," writes Julie Wheelwright in *The Fatal Lover: Mata Hari and the Myth of Women in Espionage*.

• Suspicious about her movements, the British warned the French, who arrested Mata Hari on February 13, 1917. She was shot on October 15, despite her protestations of innocence and her 75-year-old lawyer's cunning plan to save her life by claiming he had got her pregnant.

• She died bravely. When leaving Saint-Lazare prison for execution, she looked at the crowd and exclaimed: "All these people! What a success!" (Other sources: *Sunday Telegraph*, *Great Mysteries of the Past*.)

The axis and entertainment

In August 1991, the 53-year-old businessman Hidekatsu Tojo finally launched his career as a professional singer. He is a grandson of Prime Minister Hideki Tojo, who was hanged for war crimes (and has been labelled Japan's Hitler). The would-be pop star's first hit song was a war requiem; Mr. Tojo said he postponed his career for 30 years because of the "Tojo allergy."
• Romano Mussolini, youngest son of dictator Benito Mussolini, became a jazz pianist. In 1964, he told a Toronto press conference: "I think my father was a great man and I am convinced he was against the war." When legendary jazz trumpeter Chet Baker met Mr. Mussolini in Rome, he said, "Oh, yeah, man, it was a drag about your dad."
• Adolf Hitler lived for six months in Liverpool – which would later be the birthplace of the Mersey Beat – according to his sister-in-law, Bridget Hitler. In memoirs written during the Second World War, she says Hitler was a draft-dodger from the Austrian army and that she persuaded the "weak and spineless" young man to prune back his handlebar mustache. (The reported visit, in 1912-13 during the future dictator's "lost years," has not been confirmed.) In the 1940s, Mrs. Hitler's son Patrick visited Toronto's Massey Hall on a lecture tour and spoke about his uncle. (Sources: *Times* of London, *Jazz Anecdotes*, *Globe* files.)

For the health-conscious

• Do not use phones, showers, or baths during a thunderstorm, advises David Phillips in his book *The Day Niagara Falls Ran Dry*. (Sensing the static electricity on their fur before a storm, cats will lick and groom themselves, but this is probably safe.)

Over a recent ten-year period, 380 Australians were killed or injured by lightning while talking on the phone during a thunderstorm.
• John Peters and John Nichols, two RAF pilots knocked out of the sky by the Iraqis during the Gulf War, wrote *Tornado Down* (1992) about their experiences. They describe overhearing a U.S. pilot refuse a mug of tea from their Iraqi captors, saying, "Tea contains caffeine. It's bad for your health."

Meteor showers

The appearance of meteors is unpredictable and often dazzling. Among the best-known and spectacular showers are the Perseids, which peak in August. Some notes:
• A piece of interplanetary debris (a meteoroid) becomes a meteor if it zips through our sky and lights up, a bolide if it explodes, a meteorite if it lands. Every two hours a softball-sized meteoroid thumps to the ground, writes Paul Vance and Lee Pockriss in *Catch a Falling Star*. Hundreds more rain down worldwide as smaller pebbles.
• All but the biggest landing meteorites are slowed by the atmosphere to 320 to 650 kilometres an hour; thus they are found on the ground or in holes only slightly larger than themselves. Newly fallen meteorites are not hot to the touch, says *Sky & Telescope* magazine; they have cooled during freefall.
• Retrieved meteorites can be worth their weight in gold; a few are more valuable because they appear to have been blasted from the moon or Mars. Collecting meteorites can be as simple as laying strips of flypaper on a rooftop, but such harvests are heavily contaminated by terrestrial particles.
• On a clear night, observers can see about six meteors an hour. In November 1966, the Leonid shower produced a storm of

about 100,000 meteors an hour over the United States. Some believe the Leonids' astral fireworks on November 17, 1999, will be a highlight of the world's millennium celebrations.

Dangerous mushrooms

The fungi are out:

• Are wild mushrooms poisonous? The rule of thumb seems to be that some are, some aren't. (Scientists do not make the distinction of calling edible fungi "mushrooms" and poisonous ones "toadstools.")

• About 70 or 80 species are poisonous to humans. Although a few are deadly, most cases of illness come from the varieties that are only mildly poisonous.

• Mushrooms with gills, which include the only varieties cultivated commercially, also account for the deadliest kinds. The gills produce four colours of spores: white, rosy, purple-brown, and black. Edible species are found displaying all colours, but the most lethal have white spores. (Also, don't eat wild mushrooms in the button stage, before they can be checked for spore colour.)

• Some fallacies: mushrooms are edible if they are white or have a ring at the foot of the stalk; mushrooms that turn bluish are poisonous (it just means they are fermenting); pleasant-smelling mushrooms are edible (deadly ones can smell nice); soaking in vinegar makes a mushroom edible (deadly varieties are never safe to eat).

• Some signs that a person has eaten a bad mushroom are nausea, vomiting, and death. If in doubt, don't eat it. Mushrooms are a meagre source of nutrition, anyway. A kilogram has only 88 calories.

Geographical names

• There's a trend to give babies geographic names, wrote Peter Freedman in the *Sunday Times* of London in 1992. Mick Jagger's granddaughter is Assisi, actors Don Johnson and Melanie Griffith have named their newborn Dakota, and the granddaughter of writer Evelyn Waugh has named her baby Alabama, "because we didn't want her to sound like a librarian."

• "Eric Gotobed, Little Snoring, England" is a real person and place, says the *Wall Street Journal*, adding that England probably leads the world in peculiar place names, including Crackpot, Dorking, Fattahead, Goonbell, Giggleswick, Nether Poppleton, Wormelow Tump, and Yonder Bognie.

Born to be wild

In August 1885, a wooden bicycle powered by an internal-combustion engine was patented in Germany. Gottlieb Daimler's Einspur had a one-half horsepower engine and could reach 19 kilometres an hour. (It was an advance over an English steam-powered model exhibited in 1881.) Some notes on bikes and bikers:

• Early motorbikes appealed to the young and adventurous. They had to be started with a running push. Some engines were ignited by preheating a gas-filled tube with a flame.

• The popularity of the vehicle grew after 1910. It was used in both world wars, mainly for dispatching, and between the wars as a sport vehicle.

• Law-enforcement files show that most U.S. motorcycle gangs started in California in the 1940s when groups of military veterans had trouble settling down into civilian life. One of these associations, the Pissed Off Bastards of Bloomington, eventually became the Hell's Angels.

• In 1947, a riotous biker weekend in Hollister, California, spawned the leather-jacketed, outlaw image of riders. It also inspired the 1954 movie *The Wild One*, starring Marlon Brando.

• Japanese motorcycle gangs, the *bosozoku*, imitate the outlaw Brando look, but they ride domestic bikes. They beat up people and violate anti-noise laws.

Significant digits

• One: It takes a lot of bees to kill a human being, say U.S. scientists; the rule of thumb is that a person can withstand ten stings per pound of body weight. However, adds the *New York Times*, about 1 per cent of the population are allergic to stings and can suffer severe injury or death if a sting is not treated quickly.

• Two: With each swallow, a person takes in 3 ccs. of air, writes Daniel Kucharsky in *Family Practice* magazine. Since we swallow about 600 times in 24 hours – mostly during the daytime – that's about two litres of air daily.

• Three: Humid weather, says Environment Canada, can make hair about 3 per cent longer. A person's head grows a total of seven miles of hair annually; your mileage may differ.

• 4.5: Long car trips can be hard on people's backs, according to experts. "The problem is that our spines vibrate at a natural frequency of about 4.5 cycles per second, and when we encounter an environment where vibrations duplicate the natural frequency, we're in trouble," says Dr. Malcolm Pope, director of orthopaedic research at the University of Vermont. "It's comparable to the effect of an opera singer who can shatter a crystal glass by singing a note that duplicates the natural frequency of the glass."

• Eight: One in eight Canadians can expect at least one hospital stay for mental illness.

• Ten: The average life span of a face lift is estimated at six to ten years.

• 13: When assessing a child's potential height, doctors have a rule of thumb, writes Gady Epstein for Knight-Ridder News. Add the parents' heights together, add 13 centimetres for boys or subtract the same for girls, and divide by two.

• 40: The average age of death for frequent users of heroin is 40, say researchers with the University of California at Los Angeles. Also, those who do not quit by their late 30s are unlikely ever to stop.

• 10,000: The human sense of smell is 10,000 times more sensitive than the sense of taste. A woman has a greater ability to smell than a man. North Atlantic sailors are reputed to be able to smell nearby icebergs.

• 20,000: The world's worst inflation occurred in Hungary in 1945-46; over a period of about a year, the rate was 20,000 per cent a month. By June 1946, a single 1931 gold pengo was valued at 130 quadrillion paper pengos.

The big sneeze
_____

The coming Labour Day weekend is the traditional peak of the hay fever season:

• The term "hay fever" was coined 150 years ago. The disorder does not come from hay and causes no fever. About 200 years ago, hay fever was almost unknown, yet today it is a commonplace illness around the world. Up to one-fifth of people will be afflicted at some time.

• Hay fever is ten times as common in the city as the country. It is virtually unknown in rural areas of developing nations.

Scientists have two theories: allergies are linked to increasing pollution; allergies appear in cleaner, urban environments because people's immune systems – no longer battling daily assaults from parasites or other invaders – need something such as pollen to battle.

• Ragweed is one of the world's more potent allergens, and its pollen can travel up to 300 kilometres. Ontario is the worst area in the world for ragweed-caused hay fever; the soil and climate in southern Ontario are perfect for the plant.

The tabloids say ...

• Husband kills nagging wife with booby-trapped cat (*Weekly World News*).
• Businessman beats stress by running inside "hamster wheel" (*Sun*).
• Con sends death notes to judges after learning to write in prison (*National Enquirer*).
• Baby walks after sipping a brew (*National Examiner*).
• Killer talks mother into taking rap for murder he committed (*Sun*).
• Hitler living in Brazil – with his gay lover (*Weekly World News*).

Thought du month

"Summer afternoon – summer afternoon; to me those have always been the two most beautiful words in the English language." – U.S. novelist Henry James (1843-1916) in *A Backward Glance*.

September

Parliamentary usage

On September 1, 1905, Alberta and Saskatchewan entered Confederation as provinces. Albertans who follow parliamentary debates know that, among the 172 words and phrases forbidden nowadays to members of its provincial legislature is "fat wingless ducks." Notes on political speech:

• It is not always polite. In 1990, for instance, Canadian senators were swapping cries of "dictator," "shame," and "despicable little bugger." Thus, when parliamentarians debate, there must be rules for language, based on previous speakers' rulings.

• Although every parliament has its own forbidden language, the terms "liar" and "lying" are universally condemned. Personal attacks are also frowned upon.

• Ottawa's forbidden list includes: bag of wind, blatherskite, dim-witted saboteur, pompous ass, political sewerpipe, small and cheap, lacking in intelligence, crook, evil genius, Nazi, and trained seal. Words that have been allowed include coward, cynic, obscene, rotten, stupid, and phony.

• Ontario has rejected vultures, crazies, and boring.

• Australia's senator Peter Walsh was forced to withdraw offensive remarks 48 times during the period 1976-89. His repartee included: "What's this gurgle I hear from the one-man gutter-slime on my left?"

• Banned phrases around the world: anthill politics (Zambia), dingo (Australia), Castro lover (Bermuda), bloodsuckers (Lesotho), change colours like a chameleon (India), and representative of the drinking class (New Zealand).

Of pigeons past . . .

On September 1, 1914, Martha died and fell off her perch at the Cincinnati zoo. She was 29. The passenger pigeon was the second pigeon species to become extinct thanks to humans. Some notes:

• The dodo of Mauritius was a dove, zoologically – and it resembled a big, ugly pigeon the size of a turkey. By 1681, within 100 years of the discovery of the species, the last one had been clubbed to death. "Up to that point," writes a naturalist, "it hadn't really clicked with man that an animal could cease to exist."

• Some dodos had been taken to Europe. The totally tame creatures were a sensation – few sights or sounds seemed to distract them. No one thought to breed them.

• By 1755, the islanders of Mauritius could not even remember the dodo. Europeans of the time refused to believe that such a fantastic-looking bird had ever existed. In 1863, several complete skeletons were painstakingly assembled; experts conceded that the dodo had been real.

• When Europeans came to North America, the continent had billions of passenger pigeons. In 1800, the species accounted for one-third of the world's bird population. A flock could take three days to pass overheard. Where it roosted, trees broke under the birds' weight and vegetation was devastated by their droppings.

• Because the pigeons were good eating (in 1648, they saved the New England Pilgrims from starvation), tons were slaughtered by pioneers and shipped east to New York.

• Some hunters boasted of killing 10,000 a day. Smudge pots suffocated them at night. Some people stood on hilltops and clubbed them out of the sky. A captured passenger pigeon, with its eyes sewn shut, was sometimes staked out to attract others by its cries. This was the "stool pigeon."

• In 1900, a young Ohio boy testing a new air rifle shot the last passenger pigeon in the wild. He didn't recognize what he had killed. (Sources: *Our Fascinating Earth*, Panati's *Extraordinary Endings*, *Globe* files.)

Labour Day

In 1894, Canada and the United States made the first Monday in September a holiday. Americans have erected a statue to New York's Peter J. McGuire, a founder of the Brotherhood of Carpenters and Joiners, as "the founder of Labour Day," but this labour tradition is much older and more Canadian than usually thought:

• In 1834, one of the first labour parades occurred in London, to protest against the conviction of the Tolpuddle Martyrs, six farm labourers who had attempted to form a union. Fifty thousand protesters walked to Whitehall to present a petition to the home secretary. He refused it. (In 1844, five of the six Tolpuddle victims emigrated to London, Ontario, where they lived for many years in obscurity.)

• In 1872, Canada declared Monday, April 15, a Day of Thanksgiving for the recovery of the Prince of Wales from typhoid fever. Taking advantage of this holiday, the Toronto Trades Assembly organized a parade of four marching bands and 3,000 workers from 13 unions. There was a printer's strike in the city – unionists were demanding a 54-hour week. The aim of the demonstration was to secure the freedom of members of the typographical union who had been charged with belonging to a union. (Unionizing did not become legal in Canada until June 14 of that year.) The *Globe*'s publisher, George Brown, was a principal target of protesters.

• Having an annual parade and picnic became a Toronto labour tradition. In 1882, unionists invited New York's Peter McGuire to be one of the speakers after the parade; he declined, citing his ailing wife and wishing Toronto a good "festival."

• On May 8 of that year, Mr. McGuire rose at a meeting of the Noble Order of the Knights of Labour to propose a day of celebration for labour in New York that would show workers' strength and *esprit de corps*. He suggested sometime between July 4 and the U.S. Thanksgiving.

• The Knights of Labour were a moderate reform movement whose objectives included an eight-hour day and abolition of child labour. Alexander Wright, editor of their journal, was a journalist from Markham, Ontario, who had worked in Guelph before going south. He argued for a festive day that was distinct from May 1, which was observed in Europe as a labour day and already associated with radicalism.

• On September 5, 1882, New York unionists marched. The parade became a tradition that spread to other U.S. centres.
• Mr. Wright returned to Canada to lobby for a labour day. It is thought that politicians of both countries adopted the September holiday because, among other things, North Americans needed a long weekend at the end of summer. (Sources: *Globe* files, *The Canadian Encyclopedia*, *The Chronicle of Canada*, *Encyclopedia Britannica*.)

Significant digits

• One: Most North Americans eat about a kilogram of insects a year, according to Michael Burgett, an entomologist at Oregon State University. The bugs are ground up into invisibly small chunks in items such as  strawberry jam, peanut butter, spaghetti sauce, apple sauce, and frozen chopped broccoli.
• 3.2: The average mother worldwide has about 3.2 children in her lifetime, down from 5.0 in the 1950s.
• 29: A safety official with Boeing estimates that someone born on a U.S. aircraft in the 1980s and remaining on board perpetually as it was operated would live to be 2,300 years old before being involved in an accident. Then, he or she would have a 29 per cent chance of surviving the mishap.
• 36: If all 5.5 billion people on Earth were gathered together in Prince Edward Island and given 60-centimetre squares to stand on, they would occupy only 36 per cent of the island and it would be 1,000 years before they would have to move on to a larger province.
• 200,000: "Saccades" – short, jerky movements of the eyeballs several times a second – are the fastest movements

humans can make. People make 100,000 to 200,000 saccades daily, reports the University of Rochester.

A cold and bitter war

The Cold War began on September 5, 1945, when a Ukrainian cipher clerk walked out of the Soviet Embassy in Ottawa with 109 documents stashed under his shirt. Igor Gouzenko, 26, held evidence that the Soviets had been spying in Canada since 1924. Information about the atomic bomb was their priority; the Soviets also got important information about radar and other technologies.

• At first, no one took the clerk seriously. Ottawa's justice minister was told that Gouzenko was in his office. "I cannot see him," said Louis St. Laurent. "I cannot take any part in a quarrel between an employee in the embassy and his employers. After all, this might become a rather serious international incident."

• Gouzenko showed up at the offices of the *Ottawa Journal* at 11 P.M. Chester Frowde, the night editor, tried for ten minutes to understand the nervous man's ramblings. He then directed Gouzenko to the RCMP, telling a colleague, "There goes a man who either has a big story or is a kook."

• Gouzenko spent 40 anxious hours on the streets of Ottawa, dodging an attempt on September 7 by the Soviet secret police to grab him.

• Eventually, his papers helped convict a dozen Canadian spies, including Fred Rose, a Communist member of parliament, and scientists working on classified military projects. In his first formal statement, October 10, Gouzenko charged that Moscow was preparing for a third world war.

• There was no Soviet ambassador to Canada from 1945-53. In Moscow, there was no Canadian ambassador during 1946-54.
• Fred Rose spent four years in prison and, upon his release, returned to his native Poland. He was bitter about losing his Canadian citizenship.

Robin Hood: Robbing hood

September 8 is the birthday of King Richard the Lionhearted (1157-1199), for years a popular and heroic figure in the medieval Robin Hood legend, among others. Modern historians view the king less kindly. Robin Hood has escaped much revisionist criticism. However:
• There were many Robin Hoods; the name was a medieval version of "John Doe" used by criminals.
• The Robin Hood of legend lived in the 13th century, many years after King Richard was dead. Whoever he was, he robbed the rich and poor alike and gave to himself. In the 13th century, only one in 100 murderers was ever caught; the rest commonly took to the woods as outlaws.
• The "merry" men were actually "meyne" ("many") men. Friar Tuck was probably two different people combined. The Elizabethans, fond of nobility in heroes, likely elevated Robin Hood to Earl of Huntingdon.
• Sherwood Forest was mostly grasslands in the 13th century. The oak trees in the area were just acorns in Robin Hood's time.
• Nottingham, with 290,000 population, attracts a million tourists a year to its Sherwood Forest Village Centre. A few years ago, a local pamphlet debunking the Robin Hood myth was burned by the Sheriff of Nottingham. (Sources: Info Globe, news agencies, *Encyclopedia Britannica*.)

It's an honour

In the fall, a list of appointments to the Order of Canada is announced. This honour, created in 1967, has three ranks – companion, officer, and member – and a Latin motto meaning "they desire a better country."

• Honours are roughly divided into "orders," for people with a common distinction, and "decorations" or medals. The oldest orders are Spanish.

• Canada's first distinctively national honour, the Canada Medal, was authorized in 1943 but never bestowed. Prime Minister Mackenzie King was given a list of nominees but, opposed to an honours system, thought the better of it.

• Inflation can devalue decorations. In the 1983 invasion of Grenada, 7,000 American troops were awarded 8,600 medals.

• Notable world orders have included: Order for Service to the Austrian Republic (13 classes); Bolivia's National Order of the Condor of the Andes; Taiwan's Order of the Precious Tripod; the Order of a Million Elephants, Laos; the Order of the White Elephant, Thailand; the Order of Chastity second class, Ottoman Turkey. (Sources: Info Globe, *Canadian*, *Canadiana*, and *Americana* encyclopedias.)

World o' animals

September 16 is Independence Day in Mexico. When Spanish conquistador Hernan Cortes reached Mexico City in 1519, he discovered that the Aztecs had a magnificent zoo, says the *Encyclopedia Britannica*. Their collection, which included birds of prey, mammals, and reptiles, was so large that it required a staff of 300 keepers. Here are some animals you may see at the zoo, at home, offshore, or in your nightmares:

• Giraffes: The world's tallest animal; perhaps the tallest mammal that ever existed. Pumping blood 3.5 metres up to the brain requires a massive heart with walls that are seven-centimetres thick. The animal's neck arteries and veins are a complicated series of valves and a so-called "wonder net" that regulate pressure. Among other things, this prevents a giraffe from blowing its brains out when it bends down to drink. Giraffes are nervous and not too bright. Their endearing qualities include: weeping, uttering low moans or whistles, and the ability to eat Christmas trees.

• Elephants: African tuskers sometimes roll in red clay to rid themselves of parasites, thus becoming pink elephants. With gestation and nursing, a female elephant can be receptive for mating only a few days every four or five years. Males spend a part of each year in an irritable condition.

• Koalas: "Koalas are not particularly cuddly," says Frank Carrick, a zoologist at Queensland University in Australia. "If you try to pick one up in the wild it may attack. They are quite powerful, with big claws and very effective teeth. You are quite likely to have your ear ripped off."

• Piranhas: A misunderstood fish; most of the 30 species are relatively harmless, surviving on fruits and seeds floating in South American rivers and rarely nipping at people. However, they have razor-sharp teeth and attack people who venture too close to their nests.

• Pandas: Although pandas are the world's symbols of cuteness and environmental concern, the keepers at Washington's National Zoo describe their own bear, the popular female Ling-Ling, as being about as cuddly as a piranha. In 1984, she woke up and rushed her keeper, gnawing his neck, leg, and hand as well as clawing his back when he tried to clean her cage. "It was her first chance to get me," he told the *Washington Post* magazine.

• Octopuses: British psychologist Stuart Sutherland, who has studied them, says, "There was one beast that particularly intrigued me. As I approached its tank, it would swim towards the surface. Having anchored itself to the side of the tank and filled its mantle with water, it would raise its siphon above the surface and blast a strong jet of sea water into my face. It would then retreat to the bottom of its tank, where it would roll about."

• Rats: When a woman in New York discovered she had rats, she tried to win them over by serving them cereal and singing to them. Before long, said Mohamed Soliman of the Lower East Side rat-prevention centre, "they slept in the bed, she slept in a chair. . . . When you provide rats with food, that's it."

• Gryphons: The gentle gryphon in *Alice in Wonderland* was based on one of the most fearsome of animals in mythology, an eagle-headed/lion-bodied creature that may have been real, reports the *Sunday Telegraph*. Scientists reconstructing a Titanis from a fossil beak believe it was a flightless, four-metre-high bird that could run faster than a racehorse and dismember any animal it caught. The Titanis was the "most dangerous bird that ever existed," says Larry Marshall of the Institute of Human Origins in Berkeley, California. The species walked around the world from South America in the last ice age, and legends of gryphons or dragons guarding their treasures might derive from Titanis guarding its eggs and young from humans.

Shine on harvest moon

The full moon nearest the autumnal equinox is called the harvest moon because it extends the hours of light, helping harvesters with their long day's work. It also helps students, just returned to school, to work longer into the night on their homework – and that's a remark to be expected of a "mooncalf," or dolt. Some other words that show the moon's influence:

• Moonchild: a person born under the zodiacal sign of Cancer, a favourite of hippies in the late 1960s.

• Moonshine: a term for illegal home-brew liquor but, in the 15th century, a term for foolishness.

• Moonrakers: simpletons, named after the liquor-smuggling yokels of Wiltshire, England, who supposedly raked a pond to capture the reflected moon; thus, feigning stupidity before tax officials.

• Moonlighting: holding a night job (North America), taking additional employment (Britain and North America), riding after cattle (Australia), agrarian violence by night (Ireland, in former times).

• Moon-blink: temporary blindness caused by sleeping in tropical moonlight.

• Mooner: A person who gives police a hard time and is believed to be the most pesky during a full moon.

• Peter Moon: An active *Globe and Mail* reporter.

• Mooning: To expose one's buttocks, as an insult. The practice began in the United States in the 1950s but was also traditional among the Maori. (Sources: *Wicked Words*, *Slang!*, and various Oxford dictionaries.)

The cartoon moralist

September 27 is the birthday of George Cruikshank (1792-1878), an eminent Victorian artist, caricaturist, and illustrator. Some notes:

• The son of an artist, Cruikshank became popular in his teens with his biting caricatures for a magazine called *The Scourge, A Monthly Expositor of Imposture and Folly.*

- With his sometimes-savage caricatures, Cruikshank was aiming at "moral comedies." The noted satirist attacked Tories, Whigs, George IV, Anglican liturgy, high life, low life, abuse of orphans, and England's enemies abroad – he was a staunch patriot.

- Cruikshank produced drawings for more than 850 books – he shares the credit for creating the first illustrated children's books.

- In the later decades of his life, Cruikshank was a model of Victorian rectitude, denouncing his earlier fondness for "late nights, blue ruin (gin) and the dollies." He campaigned enthusiastically against alcohol.

- On his deathbed, Cruikshank said, "Oh, what will become of my children?" This surprised his wife, because neither she nor his long-dead first wife had borne him any offspring.

- It transpired that three streets away from his London home, Cruikshank had another household, with a mistress and 11 children. She was called Adelaide, a maid who began working for the Cruikshanks in 1850. After Cruikshank's stern Presbyterian mother died in 1853, the 61-year-old illustrator began visiting her, up in her room.

- There was strong affection between Mrs. Cruikshank and Adelaide, recalled a daughter of the maid in 1992, but when the servant became pregnant and wouldn't reveal who the father was, she was dismissed.

- Cruikshank set Adelaide up in a house a few minutes' walk away. He fathered his last child with her when he was 82.

- Mrs. Cruikshank visited her former maid – a woman she

hadn't seen for almost 25 years – and insisted on helping her financially. This remained a secret, writes John Wardroper in the *Independent on Sunday*, because Cruikshank had to remain a paragon. As *Punch* stated in its obituary: "There never was a purer, simpler, more straightforward or altogether more blameless man. His nature had something childlike in its transparency." (Sources: various encyclopedias.)

Beware of mad dogs

On September 28, 1895, Louis Pasteur died. The French scientist became a medical hero in 1885 by injecting nine-year-old Joseph Meister with an experimental vaccine after the boy had been bitten by a mad dog; the child survived. In 1940, the devoted Mr. Meister committed suicide rather than obey German orders to open Pasteur's crypt in Paris.

Medical watch

• Short, intense bursts of exercise may help defuse premenstrual tension, says Dr. Peter Vash, an endocrinologist with the University of California at Los Angeles. He suggests such activities as three minutes with a punching bag.

• More Americans over 65 are hospitalized for alcoholism than for heart attacks, says a study in the *Journal of the American Medical Association*. Researchers say concern has long been muted by the belief that drinking and its problems decline in old age; they add that alcohol should be suspected as a factor when there are unexplained changes in mental function or stomach and intestinal problems.

The tabloids say ...

• Cheap guide-dog chases car three blocks – as blind miser hangs on for dear life (*Weekly World News*).
• Lost dog recognizes his owner on TV (*National Enquirer*).
• New York robber surrenders after seven-hour lecture from Jewish granny (*National Examiner*).
• UFO brain surgery turns janitor into a math genius (*Sun*).
• Marilyn Monroe's secret wish list – she had the hots for Albert Einstein (*National Enquirer*).
• Crook is too ugly to be put on wanted poster (*Sun*).
• Daredevil teens risking their lives to spraypaint elephants (*Weekly World News*).

Thought du month

"Life is hell. There are very few moments of happiness. I feel that when one experiences one of them, it is right to enjoy it. Cheers, everybody." – English playwright Harold Pinter proposes a toast at his stepson's wedding in 1992.

O c t o b e r

An unloved child

On October 3, 1931, Universal Studios finished shooting *Frankenstein*. Some notes about the motion picture that is continually one of the top 100 video rentals:

• After the surprising hit of *Dracula* earlier that year, Universal wanted another film that would feature the Hungarian actor Bela Lugosi – minus his loopy accent. They bought a theatrical adaptation of Mary Shelley's novel. (The chief difference is a relatively mute monster; the book's creature is a gas-bag who has monologues running for pages.)

• The actor, who saw himself as a romantic lead, hated the makeup and the role. He said, "I was a star in my country. . . . Anybody can moan and grunt."

• In the studio cafeteria, director James Whale noticed a fellow Briton: Boris Karloff. (Born William Pratt, Karloff was a black sheep from an unloving family of diplomats. His parents died when he was a child; he was raised by siblings. He took his acting name from a maternal relative.)

• Karloff's acting, a black-and-white film that was tinted green, and a shocking story (for the time) created a hit film.

• After test screenings, Universal cut one sadistic scene in which the monster, thinking a friendly little girl will float, throws her into a lake. (Ironically, little Marilyn Harris enjoyed being chucked into the water by Karloff. In real life, her adoptive mother – who picked her out of an orphanage for her looks, motivated her acting with beatings and other sadism, writes critic Forrest Ackerman.)

• Karloff said later he got much sympathetic fan mail, especially from children, who said they understood the monster's feelings.

• Nineteen-year-old Mary Shelley started her novel after hearing a discussion about life between her husband-to-be, Percy Shelley, and Lord Byron. Mary's mother died 11 days after giving birth (Mary was courted on her mother's gravestone) and she was raised by a cruel father who barely tolerated her. Critics have noted the parallel between her childhood and the monster's life. (Sources: *Behind the Scenes*, *The Dead That Walk*, *Universal Filmscripts*, news services.)

Shocked by a red moon

October 4, 1957, saw the dawn of the space age. As the wire report from Moscow stated, "Russia announced today it has sent the world's first artificial moon streaking around the globe 560 miles (900 kilometres) out in space." It was the height of the Cold War; the world was electrified. Some Western experts said the satellite couldn't be seen from Earth (in fact, it was visible as a dull-red orbiting dot, but was often confused with its brighter launch rocket); it would last for years in orbit (it lasted 92 days); it was spying on and mapping the Earth (it wasn't); space travel by humans was still a long way off (it was only three years away).

Swordsman, actress

October 5 is the birthday of the Chevalier d'Eon (1728-1810), one of the most famous transvestites in history and probably one of the few male diplomats to have become an actress. A few notes:

•   Charles-Genevieve-Louise-Auguste-Andrée-Timothée d'Eon de Beaumont was a short and plump Frenchman, with a soft face and voice, writes Marjorie Garber in her book *Vested Interests*. Although he dressed like a man at school, when d'Eon was sent to Russia in 1755 he is said to have assumed the dress of a woman to spy on the Empress Elizabeth – and to have returned to Russia next year, posing as a brother of himself.

• In 1759, he served with the French army and was wounded.

• When he was sent to England in 1762 as a minister plenipotentiary, d'Eon's appearance and dress aroused much debate. The London Stock Exchange took bets on his gender; the chevalier reportedly feared he would be kidnapped by interested bettors wanting to settle the question.

• In 1775, France's new king, Louis XVI, sent an envoy to persuade the chevalier to return. Instead, d'Eon persuaded the envoy he was actually a woman sent to England by Louis XV to spy in women's garb, and received a pension. However, the new king ordered him not to wear his dragoon's uniform anymore and "to dress according to her sex."

• A brilliant swordsman, says *The Pan Book of Dates*, d'Eon continued to give exhibitions as a female fencer. He was badly wounded in 1796.

• When he died in 1810, his companion of many years – a Mrs. Cole – was reportedly astounded to learn she had been living with a man.

Significant digits

• One: A heavy object dropped into the ocean over the Mariana Trench in the Pacific would take more than one hour to reach the bottom.

• Two: Top-notch flirters realize that "the first step is to stare at people," says Rich Gosse of San Francisco. "You can't be ambiguous about it. You stare for exactly two seconds. Anything less doesn't work. Anything more, they may call the cops on you." (A hint for cautious Canadians: Count "one Saskatchewan, two Saskatchewan.")

• 23: When there are 23 people in the room, there is an even chance that at least two of them share a birthday; when there are 367 people, it is a certainty.

• Four: Psychological research shows that "kissing up" to the boss gives a worker a 4 to 5 per cent advantage over a colleague who relies solely on job performance to achieve success.

• Six: The average yawn lasts about six seconds. In 1984, U.S. physician Perry Buffington pointed out that people who are acutely ill yawn less while their condition remains serious – and psychotic individuals hardly ever yawn.

• 27: Sir Alexander Korda (1893-1956), the Hungarian-born father of the modern British film industry, was a tortured man, according to BBC filmmakers. Every day for 27 years – after he divorced his first wife, to the day he died – Sir Alexander opened and read an abusive letter from her.

• 40: Sexual daydreaming peaks in men and women between 17 and 23 and drops off precipitously at 40, says psychiatrist Harold Lief of the University of Pennsylvania school of medicine.

• 100 million: Malaria-carrying mosquitoes infect about 100 million people annually and two million of them – mostly children and old people – die. In many parts of the Third World, people are bitten by malaria-bearing mosquitoes every night. In May 1975, the World Health Organization in Geneva declared "malaria has been licked." On the day of the announcement, the WHO's deputy director-general, Dr. Thomas Lambo, was rushed to hospital with malaria.

Thanksgiving Day

The harvest festival of Thanksgiving – in Canada, the second Monday in October – has wandered around the calendar more than most holidays:

• The first North American celebration was in Canada's eastern Arctic in 1578, by explorer Martin Frobisher.

• New England's Pilgrims celebrated their first Thanksgiving in autumn 1621, with turkey, squash, and pumpkin. This festival was brought to Canada as early as 1750. Abraham Lincoln made it an official U.S. holiday in 1863.

• From 1819 to 1921, Canada's official Thanksgiving was November 6. In 1931, it reverted to the second or third Monday in October, except for 1935 when it was held on a Thursday. In 1957, Ottawa formalized the present date.

Northward, ho

October 15, 1920, saw the first commercial airplane flight to Canada's North, from Winnipeg to The Pas, Manitoba. The passenger had to help the pilot and flight engineer with the trip.

Two weeks in October

On October 15, 1962, U.S. intelligence experts, studying films taken by a U-2 spy plane over Cuba, were surprised to see a Soviet missile-launching area. When the public heard about a U.S. blockade of Cuba on October 22, they didn't know the full story. Neither did Washington nor Moscow:

• Nikita Khrushchev, concerned about U.S. missiles in Turkey, had persuaded Fidel Castro to accept missiles in Cuba as a defence against U.S. invasion.

• The Soviet Union had 45 missiles in Cuba. Years later, the West learned that nine of them were "tactical" nukes – each with the power of the Hiroshima bomb – that could be fired at the discretion of the local Soviet commander. (At the time, U.S. missiles in Europe were controlled by their local commanders, and the ICBMs were later discovered to have electronic faults that could have caused them to launch themselves.)

• On October 22, a B-52 strayed over Siberia and was ordered destroyed. Officers in Moscow watched by radar as a pair of MiG-17s converged on the target; 50 kilometres from the bomber, they turned back. They were low on fuel.

• On October 23, Gen. Curtis LeMay, with the U.S. joint chiefs of staff, said, "If there is to be war, there's no better time than at present. We are prepared and 'the bear' is not."

• On the night of October 25, a wild bear climbed over the perimeter fence of the U.S. air force base in Duluth, Minnesota. A sentry shot at the shadowy figure and sounded the sabotage alarm to alert bases throughout the region. However, at Volk Field, Wisconsin, the alarm for nuclear war was triggered. Air crew, who had been told there would be no practice alerts during this crisis, rushed to take off. Luckily, the base commander phoned Duluth to find out what had really happened (the "saboteur" wasn't identified until later) and subordinate officers drove a car onto the Volk Field runway, blocking any departures.

• On October 26, saying "only lunatics or suicides" wanted nuclear war, Khrushchev offered to pull his missiles in return for a no-invasion pledge. But Cuban troops knocked down a U-2 and killed the pilot; U.S. fliers assumed they would hit back; however, Kennedy said, "We shall try (negotiations) again."

• On October 27, which was the deadline for Soviet missiles to be operational, a deal was reached and announced on Moscow Radio. U.S. troops had been scheduled to invade Cuba on October 29. (Sources: *Eyeball to Eyeball*, *The Limits of Safety*, *Independent on Sunday*, news services.)

Duelling

On October 17, 1878, Sir John A. Macdonald became prime minister of Canada for the second time. In 1838 or 1839, Sir John served as the second in a duel and was dissuaded from fighting a duel of his own in 1849. Duelling has a long history:
• Judicial duels began in 6th-century Burgundy, as trial by combat to learn the "judgment of God." As recently as 1817, an accused murderer in Britain had to be acquitted because he

chose the right to "wage his battle" over trial by jury, and no one wanted to fight him.

• On the European continent, the challenger in a personal duel had the right to choose the weapons, usually swords or pistols. In English-speaking countries, the challenged party had this right. In 1843, billiard balls were the weapons in a fatal duel fought in France.

• Duels were fought in New France as early as 1646. The last recorded fight in what is now known as Canada took place in St. John's in 1873. The death toll in the years between: at least nine in New France, two in Lower Canada, five in Upper Canada, two each in Nova Scotia and New Brunswick, and one in Newfoundland.

• The last legal duel in Canada was fought on the campus of Dalhousie University in 1816. Although such encounters were considered a crime, Canadian juries consistently refused to convict duellists if they thought the fights had been fair.

The kamikazes

On October 19, 1944, Japanese vice-admiral Takajiro Ohnishi asked 23 young navy pilots to volunteer for suicide missions against Allied warships; those who crashed into aircraft carriers would get posthumous double promotions. They all agreed, creating the first "special attack group" in time for the Battle of Leyte Gulf, which began the next day. Notes on Japan's kamikaze attacks:

• Some suicide fliers were volunteers, others under orders. There were kamikaze boats and rafts.

• By October 25, the U.S. navy realized that suicide crash landings on its ships were not just being improvised. It clamped a news blackout on kamikaze fliers and began to figure out how to deal with their strategies (such as their habit of tailing a group of American aircraft back home to the carrier). One in every four kamikaze flights inflicted damage, and the navy was seriously concerned that Tokyo not find out the success of its tactical surprise.

• A hero during the indoctrination of the kamikaze pilots, sailors, and swimmers was naval warrant officer Magoshiche Sugino. Japanese believed that he had given his life in 1904, during the Russo-Japanese war, while sinking a ship to bottle up the Russian fleet at Port Arthur. In 1946, he was discovered living quietly in Manchuria. Mr. Sugino had been rescued by a Chinese boat and, upon learning he was a dead hero, decided to keep a low profile.

Medical watch

• "If you were going to have a heart attack today, the chances are you would already have had it," writes Robert Matthews in the *Sunday Telegraph*. He notes that heart attacks peak in the morning, when the blood's platelets are more likely to clump together.

• Sleep research suggests that window-shopping or spending time under a hair dryer could help hardened insomniacs far more than counting sheep. Psychologists believe warming the brain by increasing its visual workload during the day makes it easier for people to fall into deep sleep at night.

• The dedication of runners can be excessive, reports the *Boston Globe*. For instance, Dr. Lyle Micheli of that city's Children's Hospital remembers treating a man who collapsed a few metres before the end of the Boston Marathon. He had suffered pain in his leg halfway through the event but had pressed on. When the leg was examined, it was ten centimetres shorter than its mate; the man had been running on a major fracture.

• "The most common cause of death for people with Alzheimer's is pneumonia," says Michael Russell, the head of an aging study at the University of California. He told the *Los Angeles Times*, "They die as a result of being bedridden and immobile. You can lose almost all of the cortical layer of your brain and survive. But people can't stay bedridden for long."

Down with the chute

There were many 18th-century experiments with parachutes; they included sheep chucked out of towers and dogs dropped from hot-air balloons. The first true parachutist, André Garnerin, jumped from a balloon on October 22, 1797:

• Parachutes were not only dangerous for their numerous pioneers, they were also seen as vulgar – balloonists associated them with circuses and showing off.

• In the First World War, when German pilots began to use parachutes to avoid a stricken aviator's dilemma – burning to death or jumping – Allied pilots had second thoughts. (The first German to use a chute waved happily at the French pilot who'd shot his aircraft, but was wounded 27 times from groundfire in no-man's land.)

• Humans reach about 190 kilometres an hour "terminal velocity" when jumping (320 kilometres an hour if they rocket down headfirst). With a parachute, speed drops to about 16 to 22 kilometres an hour.

• Some pilots have survived drops where their parachutes failed utterly – when, for example, they landed in deep snow. Sir Brian Urquhart survived a dud chute in 1942 over Salisbury

Plain: "I noticed I was falling somewhat rapidly. My sergeant waved at me and shouted, 'So long, sir!' as I passed him on the way down." Sir Brian suffered a broken back and legs but lived to become a top official with the United Nations. (Sources: *The Silken Angels, Encyclopedia Britannica*, others.)

Beginnings and ends

• October 23, 4004 BC, at 6 P.M., the world was created, according to 17th-century archbishop James Ussher of Ireland, who added together the ages of the men cited in the Old Testament's "begats." (Some references claim that this cleric designated October 26 at 9 A.M.)

• Worldwide, there are at least 1,100 groups that believe the apocalypse is at hand, according to the Millennial Prophecy Report, a Philadelphia-based newsletter published by folklorist Ted Daniels. As of 1994, half a dozen messiahs around the globe were biding their time until Judgment Day.

• Psychologists' views differ about apocalyptic visions. Some think the images are just a recollection of the birth trauma (earthquakes, seas and rivers running with blood, the sky in chaos, et cetera). However, New York therapist Mortimer Ostow notes that such fantasies are often found at the beginning of psychotic episodes. "End-of-the-world fantasies are found in almost all patients who have trouble controlling rage."

Over the falls

On October 24, 1901, at 4:23 P.M., Anna Edson Taylor became the first person to go over Niagara Falls and live. The 50-year-old teacher of physical culture and dancing – today, she might be called an aerobics instructor – was trying to pay down her mortgage. Some notes from contemporary accounts:

• Mrs. Taylor was born and raised in Auburn, New York. She was married at 17 and widowed at 20.

• Her barrel was 4.5-feet high and 3-feet wide; it had a common blacksmith's anvil affixed to the bottom and, true to her calculations, the 175-pound weight kept the barrel "foot downwards," so her skull was not crushed.

• As well as using leather harnesses, Mrs. Taylor wore a strong girdle fastened to the bottom of the barrel. She put feather pillows under each arm. Her last words to assistants before the barrel was closed were: "Goodbye, boys."

• As Mrs. Taylor bobbed for a mile down the river, news of her attempt was spread to the public. Tumbling over the Horseshoe Falls was like being in a plummeting elevator. The subsequent impact knocked her breathless. The teacher prayed all the time, she recalled.

• Her first words, when the barrel was recovered and opened, were, "Where am I?" ("You are over the falls and are all right," replied Mr. Harvey Williams of the Hotel Lafayette.) The inside of the barrel was soaked.

• By ten o'clock that night, Mrs. Taylor was in hospital, being rubbed all over, every hour, with liniment. She said she wouldn't take the plunge again, even for a million dollars.

Toronto Stock Exchange

October 24, 1852, saw the founding of the Toronto Stock Exchange. Each morning, 12 businessmen met for 30 minutes, in members' offices, to trade shares. A seat on the exchange sold for $5. No trading records of the Association of Brokers survive – if, indeed, any were kept.

The birth of the box

On October 30, 1925, John Logie Baird of London transmitted his first TV picture: the head of a dummy. The Scot was one of many inventors credited with launching the medium and his technique was one of several. Some notes:

• Mr. Baird was the sort of idea-rich inventor who couldn't change a fuse by himself, but had a flair for publicity. He had previously failed at making artificial diamonds and had attempted a cure for haemorrhoids that left him in severe pain for a week. His TV camera and receiver used spinning discs, with spirals of holes, to "sample" images. (Such electromechanical systems were tried on both sides of the Atlantic.) The images were low-definition – 50 lines or so, in a picture that was often only a silhouette – but they used radio waves that could travel great distances. In 1928, Baird's team transmitted live pictures from London to New York.

• Electromechanical television enjoyed a boom from 1928 to 1933. Canada's first TV station, VE9EC in Montreal, was opened in 1931, by *La Presse*.

Keep watching the skies

Martians had a 99-year lease on life – from 1877, when an Italian astronomer reported seeing canali ("channels" – mistranslated as "canals") on the planet, to 1976, when a pair of Viking landers made biological tests and found nothing. (Previous spacecraft had dispelled the idea of canals; they were a combination of wishful thinking and optical illusion.) On October 30, 1938, Orson Welles broadcast a dramatization of H. G. Wells' *War of the Worlds*. Of the ten million people who heard the radio play, an estimated one million believed that

Martians had landed in New Jersey. Panic caused miscarriages and broken limbs. Some people hid in church basements; others roamed the highways with guns, looking for invaders. (Mr. Wells, the author, later denounced Mr. Welles.) CBC knew that the broadcast would cause trouble. Censors made 27 handwritten changes to the script, to make it less realistic, and four times during the program an announcer said, "This is purely a fictional play."

The tabloids say ...

• 18-year-old Siamese twins learn they were glued together by their mom (*Sun*).
• Boy, 12, guns down parents who made him do homework (*National Enquirer*).
• He meets future wife while sleepwalking in the nude (*Sun*).
• Groucho's wacky walk is the safest new way to work out (*News Extra*).
• How to tell if your pet's a transvestite (*National Examiner*).
• Mobster boss assassinated by exploding hemorrhoid ointment (*National Examiner*).

Thought du month

"Ten years is long enough to wait for any man." – Beatrice Houdini, in 1936, after repeated attempts to reach her dead husband, magician Harry Houdini, who died on Halloween 1926 after being punched in the stomach by a student boxer from McGill University.

November

November First

• On this day in 80,000 BC, most of Canada was covered by a sheet of glacial ice.

The truth about Marie?

Marie Antoinette, queen of France, was born on November 2, 1755. The 200th anniversary of her execution was marked in 1993 by a play titled *My Name is Marie Antoinette*; about that time, a poll indicated that the French were split over whether the woman who supposedly said "let them eat cake" should have been sent to the guillotine. The stage production concluded with an audience vote – and most people were clapping for her, said the Associated Press.

Marie Antoinette almost certainly did not make the infamous wisecrack about cake, historians agree. (The French play omits that line.) Some of what they now believe:

• Accused of being extravagant, feasting lavishly, and wearing 160 dresses a year, the queen actually invested most of her income.

• Marie Antoinette was married at 12, taught to read by her husband, and persuaded by her brother, Joseph II of Austria, to consummate her marriage at last when she was 19.

• During the endless Holy Week Masses at Versailles, Marie Antoinette passed the time by reading pornography, disguised as a prayer book. Her husband, Louis XVI, knew but turned a blind eye.

• Pressed by relatives to meddle in her country's affairs, Marie Antoinette proved to be intellectually incapable of doing so. She "was indeed stupid, unimaginative, and desperately immature," contends author-historian Pierrette Girault de Coursac.

• When the potato became popular in Europe, Marie Antoinette started a fashion craze by decorating her hair with its pretty flowers.

• "Described by some as a saint and by others as an idiot, Marie Antoinette was in reality both," says historian Francois Bluche. "But she faced up to her judges with dignity. And at the end of her life (at 37), she showed piety and true Christian humility." (Sources: *Observer*, *British GQ*, news services.)

Significant digits

• One: Although water covers 70 per cent of the Earth's surface, 97 per cent of it is too salty for use. That leaves 3 per cent to sustain life – however, 2 per cent of the planet's water is frozen in glaciers, leaving only 1 per cent in lakes, ground-water, and the atmosphere.

• Six: On average, the skin of a person's heel is six times as resistant to pain as skin elsewhere on the body, say researchers at McGill University in Montreal.

• 15: A cockroach breaks wind every 15 minutes, reports a Dutch physicist; it also continues to release methane for 18 hours after death. Insect flatulence accounts for 20 per cent of all methane emissions, and cockroaches may be among the worst bugs in contributing to the greenhouse effect.

• 24: In a 1994 survey in *Longevity* magazine, 24 per cent of women reported that sex relieved their migraines.

• 800,000: At any given moment, there are about 800,000 people aloft in airplanes, says Michael O'Rourke of Australia's New South Wales University.

A-a-a-a-a-aa-argh!

On November 3, 1954, Japanese film star Godzilla was born. Some background on this typical Scorpio:

• Japanese call the monster Gojira, which is said to be a combination of "gorilla" and the Japanese word for whale; it was an in-joke, referring to a large, gentle stagehand at Toho Studios. (By another translation, the name means "devil monster.")

• The curiously appealing monster is a Japanese contemporary legend. His first movie was an immense box-office hit with both children and adults. Popular weeklies and intellectual monthlies have carried long articles about the reptile.

• The Godzilla project began with brainstorming at Toho Studios after a joint venture in Indonesia fell through. The story of the first film combined the elements of *King Kong* with atomic attacks on Japan during the Second World War. In this film, Godzilla seemed to object vehemently to the atom bomb's effect on humanity, writes Janet Maslin in the *New York Times*, and "he has been something of a strident social critic ever since." Eventually, he became a kind of Japanese patriot with radioactive breath, a UN peace ambassador, and an environmental activist (*Godzilla versus The Smog Monster*, 1971.)

• In a score of films, roused over and over again from his watery resting place, Godzilla spends much of his time shrieking, looking puzzled and annoyed, and attacking modern technology. He has been described as resembling a child having a temper tantrum or a personification of U.S. occupation forces.

• In Japan, the first film was titled *Gojira, Terrible Creature of the Hydrogen Bomb*. For its U.S. release, the studio played down the anti-nuke message and retitled the picture *Godzilla, King of the Monsters*. It added footage of Raymond Burr, playing visiting U.S. journalist Steve Martin, who realizes he has stumbled onto a big story. Despite the popularity of this version – Godzilla made the cover of *Time* magazine – some film buffs contend the Japanese version is artistically superior or, at least, not as tacky.

• In the 1970s, Godzilla became a wimpy, single-parent monster, writes Doug Mason of Scripps Howard News. His son was named Godzooki. After 1975, he made no more pictures for a decade, confining himself to appearances at grocery stores and shopping-mall openings. At the time, the Japanese were buying $33 billion (U.S.) worth of Godzilla merchandise. In *Godzilla '85*, he was back to his mean old self and destroying Tokyo again.

Godzilla: Rules on rampaging

Toho Studios, maker of the Godzilla movies, is careful about where the big fellow rampages, says the *Miami Herald*. Some of his guidelines:

• Tokyo's imperial palace: definitely off-limits.
• Kyoto: no destruction of this city is permitted, because the buildings are designated national treasures.
• Mount Fuji: Godzilla is permitted only on the lower slopes.
• Corporate facilities: yes, if permission is obtained.
• The city of Osaka: yes; some local residents have requested it.
• Railway trains and lines: open season.
• The Tokyo Tower: this huge broadcasting tower is the most-toppled target of the big reptile. It also happens to be ugly and located near the U.S. Embassy.

Sax appeal

November 6 is the birthday, in 1814, of Antoine-Joseph (Adolphe) Sax, the Belgian who invented the saxophone. The saxophone, which has become the pre-eminent solo instrument of jazz, was designed to revolutionize the musical world when it was invented in 1840. Sax was so afraid it would be copied that he introduced the horn at a Brussels competition by playing it from behind a curtain. It was eventually patented in 1846.

What Northern Lights do

Auroras at the north and south poles are permanent features, probably more visible from a great distance out in space than the Earth itself. Canada is the best place to see Northern Lights; there is no best season or time of night to look for them:

• The commonest auroral colour is whitish green, caused when the solar wind hits atmospheric oxygen. Other colours are blue, purple, and red, a shade rarely seen outside the Arctic.

• A few people can hear the Northern Lights hissing.

• Auroras can knock out power lines. They have fooled radar systems into reporting nuclear-missile attacks.

• On a night in 1941, a giant auroral display over North America reportedly woke up seagulls on Toronto's waterfront, knocked out communication lines, and mixed rude telephone conversations with the easy-listening music of WAAT in Jersey City, New Jersey.

• In March 1989, the Northern Lights could be seen as far south as Guatemala.

United at last

On November 7, 1885, the last spike on the Canadian Pacific Railway was driven at Craigellachie, British Columbia. Some notes:

• "At twenty-two minutes past nine," wrote the *Globe*'s correspondent, "everything was in readiness to complete the connection." Donald Smith, a fur trader/financier/politician and an important backer of the railway project, was invited to make the link. He "took the maul in hand to drive the last spike, and after missing it a few times he drove it home amid cheers from all present." When completed, the line stretched 4,653 kilometres, from Port Moody, British Columbia, to Montreal.

• "Nothing could ever be the same again," writes Pierre Berton in *The Last Spike*, "because for the first time Canadians would be able to travel the length of their nation without setting foot in a foreign land."

Cold, hard facts

Although they can occur at any time of year, this is the traditional season for catching a cold. Some notes:
• A cold incubates from one to four days; on average, the total time people spend with colds is nine days. The odds are three in four that a person will have a cold in the next 12 months.
• Children are more likely than adults to catch colds. According to U.S. figures, children aged 1 to 5 average 6 to 12 respiratory illnesses (primarily colds) a year; people older than 20 average only 3 or 4.
• Kissing rarely transmits colds, writes Carol Rinzler in *Feed a Cold, Starve a Fever*, because the cold viruses do not live comfortably in the mouth, which is cooler than the nasal passages.
• Most researchers believe that while it is polite to cover the nose or mouth when sneezing, this probably doesn't stop the spread of a cold unless the hands are washed afterward; one way people spread colds is by direct contact.
• Colds are actually quite difficult to catch, according to Dr. Elliot Dick, professor of preventive medicine at the University of Wisconsin. It takes a fairly severe cold and several hours of close contact to transmit the disease.
• There is no cure for the common cold.

In Flanders Fields

On May 3, 1915, about 7 A.M., it was a bright spring morning near Poperinghe, Belgium – the first spring of the First World War. The sky was deep blue, the larks were singing and circling, and a gentle east wind was blowing the poppies about. Maj. John McCrae, a 42-year-old doctor/soldier with the Canadian Field Artillery, was sitting on the rear step of an ambulance, composing poetry. In about 20 minutes, he wrote "In Flanders Fields." Some notes:

• The previous night, Major McCrae had buried his best friend, 25-year-old Lt. Alexis Helmer, who had been a medical student at McGill University when the poet was a professor of pathology. The young man, one of the brigade's best-liked officers, had been blown to bits by an artillery shell the previous day. (He was buried under cover of darkness for fear of attracting more enemy fire.) The barrage of The Second Battle of Ypres was in its ninth day.

• As the poet wrote, Sgt. Maj. Cyril Allinson arrived on horseback, bringing mail and supplies from the rear. "I saw (Major McCrae) sitting on the ambulance step, a pad on his knee. He looked up as I approached but continued to write," recalled Mr. Allinson, who was the first to read the work. "His face was very tired but calm as he wrote. . . . The poem was almost an exact description of the scene in front of us both."

• Major McCrae (who had been promoted to lieutenant-colonel in 1914, though the news did not reach him until June 1, 1915) made several copies of "In Flanders Fields," with slight variations, and gave them to friends. He sent a copy to *Punch* magazine, which ran the poem on December 18, 1915, with no byline.

• The verses were reprinted around the world, but the author's name was not known. By the time it was, Colonel McCrae's "perfect war poem" was famous. It has been called the best-known Canadian poem.

• Colonel McCrae, who had been at the front from the beginning, was made consultant physician to the British 1st Army in January 1918. Five days later, he was dead from pneumonia and a cerebral infection.

• "In Flanders Fields" was used in the first observance of Armistice Day in 1918, and this poem and poppies have been part of the November 11 ceremonies since. "It never occurred to me at the time that it would ever be published," Mr. Allinson admitted. "It seemed to me to be just an exact description of the scene."

Remembering the great war

Some of the dimensions of the 1914-18 war to end all wars:

• The conflict cost both sides a total of 8.5 million dead. Even on the quietest days, thousands of troops were killed or wounded – a process termed "wastage" by British officers.

• The western front soon bogged down into a stalemate from Belgium to Switzerland. Both sides built networks of trenches long enough in total, by some estimates, to circle the Earth.

• German troops built the best trenches: they picked the high ground and designed their earthworks to be permanent. Sometimes their dugouts included wallpaper and varnished woodwork. Ramshackle British and French efforts were always wet and sometimes flooded. Opposing lines could be as close as seven metres.

• The front lines, especially during winter in low-lying Flanders, were a sea of trenches, craters, latrines, corpses, and vermin. Approaching troops could smell the trenches before they saw them.

• The men were small (by modern standards) and their packs heavy. The average British recruit weighed 132 pounds and carried accoutrements of 77 pounds, including a greatcoat that might weigh 20 to 50 pounds more when soggy. Wounded men drowned by the thousands in the mud; so did unlucky sleepers.

• By 1916, both sides had steel helmets instead of cloth hats.

• The enemy was rarely seen; his bullets and shells were more common. During heavy shelling, troops endured up to 30 shells a minute – a "thunderstorm" or "symphony" of sound that was felt as much as heard. Across the English Channel, the barrages of Flanders were plainly audible.

• Informal truces sprang up when barbed wire needed mending or there were soldiers to retrieve (the wounded might moan in no man's land for days).

• Big attacks were rarely surprises; they were preceded by heavy shelling and openings of the barbed wire. On July 1, 1916, when the British attacked in the Somme, they had 60,000 casualties – one man for every 18 inches of the front.

• Record heaps of munitions were used. For instance, south of Ypres, British miners tunnelled for a year to place a million pounds of high explosives into 21 shafts. On June 7, 1917, the complex was detonated; 19 shafts went up, burying 10,000 Germans and jolting the British prime minister 130 miles away in Downing Street. In 1955, another shaft exploded, jolting the village of Ploegsteert but causing no injuries. The last shaft, deep under Ploegsteert Wood, has yet to be heard from.

• Today, bones are still being discovered. The war's battlefields will yield their metal fragments for centuries, experts say. On a rainy day in Albert, France, near the Somme, the fields give off a smell of rusting iron. (Sources: *The Great War and Modern Memory, Goodbye to All That, The First Day on the Somme, Eye-Deep in Hell.*)

Tail-Gunner Joe

November 14 is the birthday of the anti-communist U.S senator Joseph McCarthy (1908-57). From February 1950 until December 1954, he was a powerful force in Washington:
• In 1939, McCarthy began his political career as a judge in Wisconsin, after inflating his opponent's age to 89 (from 66) and reducing his own to 29 (from 31). His campaign slogan was Justice is Truth in Action.
• McCarthy was a marine from 1942 to 1944. He said he was known in the Pacific as Tail-Gunner Joe – serving on 14, then 17, then 30 missions. In 1951, he applied for, and was given, the Distinguished Flying Cross. He had only flown on a few air strikes, as a passenger when resistance was light.
• In 1946, he was elected to the Senate; his campaign slogan was Congress Needs a Tail-Gunner.
• In 1950, looking for a dramatic issue for the 1952 election, he was advised that communism was a hot topic. He made a radio speech, claiming to have a list of 205 Communists in the State Department. Surprised by the stir he caused, McCarthy later tried to get a copy of that speech to check what he had said. Ultimately, he was unable to produce a single name – this led to his downfall.
• Postwar events created sympathy for McCarthyism: Canada's Gouzenko case, the fall of China, the first Soviet atomic test, the treachery of Julius and Ethel Rosenburg, the perjury of Alger Hiss, the Korean War, Republican frustration at being out of power for two decades, and the belief Hollywood was influenced by Communists.
• It is unlikely that McCarthy had deep feelings about what he did. In 1956, at a party, he met a civil servant and former

drinking companion he had ruined and said to the man his wife was "talking about you the other night. How come we never see you? What the hell are you trying to do – avoid us?"

Feeding birds

This is the time of year when wild birds are more likely to accept food from people. The rules to keep in mind, from *Hand-Taming Wild Birds at the Feeder*:
• Always try to behave as if a bird can and does reason.
• Never approach a wild bird without speaking to it all the time.
• Always move very slowly until birds become used to your presence.
• There is no such thing as a naturally tame bird.
• Never hold out your hand unless it contains food that a bird likes.
• Never swallow while a bird is on your hand watching you.

Disney religion

Mickey Mouse made his screen début on November 18, 1928, at the Colony Theatre in New York. Some notes:
• Richard West, a cartoon historian in Washington, D.C., says Mickey's round face is the key to his personality, "which is nothing at all," writes Barbara Stewart in the *Washington Post*. "Mickey, (Mr.) West says, is so devoid of cynicism, wit or humor of any kind that he's nothing but a vacuous smile – like a New Age car salesman."
• Pati Jones of Orlando, Florida, would disagree. When interviewed by Ms. Stewart in 1993, she was dressed in a Mickey Mouse T-shirt, leggings, sneakers, and earrings – a costume she wears everywhere, except to church. Her licence plate is

MKY MUS and she carries snapshots of Mickey in her wallet. Her husband, Mark, appears tolerant of her devotion to "my Mickey son." When questioned about Minnie Mouse, Ms. Jones's voice hardens, "She's okay, I guess. But I think she gets mad at me for this."

• George Reiger of Easton, Pennsylvania, has more than 300 tattoos of Disney characters. His goal is 500, says the Orange County Register. Disneyland "is my religion. This is my life," the post-office maintenance worker said recently. "If I lived (in Anaheim), I'd come here daily. Every cent I have goes to Disney." His tattoo of Mickey Mouse is one of a handful he can't show to strangers. "My first four wives wouldn't go along with this, so they're gone."

Vamping

Being a vampire doesn't mean leading the life of a shut-in, according to Stephen Kaplan, director of the Vampire Research Center in Elmhurst, New York. "They can come out in the daytime," he told the *Los Angeles Daily News*. "They just need to wear a sun block of 15 or higher."

From hep to eternity

Jazz performer Cab Calloway, who died on November 18, 1994, was the ultimate hepcat, says the Associated Press. In the days when he performed live, he sold such how-to books as the *Hepster's Dictionary* and *Swingformation Bureau* to help square audiences collar the jive. Where do "hep" and "hip" come from? No one knows for sure, but clues abound. Some notes:

• "What puzzles me is how you can find anybody left in the world who isn't hep," says a 1908 story in the *Saturday Evening Post*.

• *The Dictionary of American Regional English* has this 1821 citation: "Today I am completely hipped. Very low spirited."

• "Hep," meaning "aware," may have been criminal slang from the name of a top-notch detective who worked in Cincinnati (1914). On the other hand, *American Speech* noted, in 1941, "'Tis said that back in the 1890s, Joe Hep ran a saloon in Chicago. . . . Although he never quite understood what was going on, he thought he did. . . . Hence his name entered the argot as an ironic appellation. . . ."

• The words "hep" and "hip" are nearly synonymous, says *The Guinness Jazz Companion*, but "hep" is slightly older. By 1945, the term "hip" had almost entirely replaced it.

• In Calloway's trademark song "Minnie the Moocher" (1931), the frail with a heart as big as a whale is taken down to Chinatown where she is shown how "to kick the gong around." A gong-kicker was an opium smoker, notes *The American Thesaurus of Slang* and, as it happens, "thin hips" was a reference to someone who has smoked dope lying on one side for so long that his hips are slightly atrophied.

Children of God . . .

On November 29, 1948, India abolished "untouchability." Mohandas Gandhi, who was assassinated earlier that year, had campaigned for decades to end the discrimination against the people he euphemistically termed Harijans (Children of God). Some notes about untouchables:

• Harijans, who make up about one-seventh of India's population, are Hindus. Their origins go back millennia: traditionally, they were leather workers, scavengers, garbage collectors, and homeless labourers. Some may have darker skins than other Hindus.

• India passed legislation in 1955 and 1976 to upgrade rights of Harijans, also known as "depressed" or "scheduled" classes. But despite a vigorous government program of quotas in parliament, the civil service, and universities, prejudice lingers.

• Harijans are often not allowed to use a town's well, enter temples, or wear shoes on certain streets. Harijan men have been persecuted for eating high-grade butter, curling their mustaches upward, and letting their wives wear ornaments.

• In recent years, some Harijans have become increasingly militant in demanding their rights. Others have converted to Christianity or Islam, where the caste system is irrelevant. (Sources: *Globe* files, *Collier's Encyclopedia*.)

...And village people

Japan has an untouchable minority, known euphemistically as *burakumin* (village people). Some notes about people previously known as *eta* (filthy), *hinan* (non-human), and *yotsu* (four-legged):

• *Burakumin* are racially and religiously identical to other Japanese, making up 1 to 2.5 per cent of the population. They were leather workers, butchers, garbage collectors, executioners, prostitutes, and street performers – as well as people who defied the emperor. They were forced to wear special clothes and were often paid with money tossed on the ground.

• As non-humans, *burakumin* were ignored by feudal lords. Their settlements were omitted from maps. In the last century, Japan acknowledged these "village people" and in 1972 began to discuss the *burakumin* in school texts.

• Since 1969, Tokyo has spent billions of dollars improving the lot of *burakumin*. However, hundreds of corporations keep computer lists to screen them out of jobs. Gangster groups sometimes claim to be *burakumin* to avoid close scrutiny. (Source: news services.)

The tabloids say ...

• Absentminded prof lives in the wrong house for a week (*Sun*).
• 65-year-old librarian works in the nude – to celebrate her retirement (*Weekly World News*).
• Demon from Hell ends up as roadkill (*Weekly World News*).
• World's bravest secretary fights bear to save boss (*National Examiner*).
• Blondes do not have more fun – they just pretend to (*Weekly World News*).

Thought du month

 "How old would you be if you didn't know how old you was?" – Satchel Paige.

December

Plinge and Spelvin

December 2 is Walter Plinge Day in England. By a long tradition, writes Richard Huggett in *The Curse of Macbeth and Other Theatrical Superstitions*, a British actor who has two parts in the same play takes the name Walter Plinge for the second role. The original Mr. Plinge may have been a theatre-crazy, 19th-century pub landlord in Drury Lane, London, who extended unlimited credit to actors – an unlikely story, if you know any actors. (Wilfred Granville, author of the definitive *Theatrical Dictionary*, says one Sunday the grateful thespians allowed Mr. Plinge to appear on stage in his own name in a benefit performance in his honour.) At the turn of the century, Walter Plinge was appearing in three West End shows simultaneously. In the United States, George Spelvin is the Plinge equivalent. His theatrical birthday is believed to be November 15, 1886, in the New York production *Karl the Peddler*. He is credited with more than 10,000 Broadway performances; his female equivalent is Georgina or Georgetta Spelvin.

Starting very early

December 5 is the anniversary of the death of Wolfgang Mozart in 1791. He was only 35 – but had started composing when he was four. When he was six, the prodigy began touring – playing the harpsichord, organ, and violin. Some accomplishments, and ages, of other early starters:

• 15: Mozart had completed his 14th symphony. Louis Braille invented his system of fingertip reading.

• 13: Mahatma Gandhi married.

• 12: Pope Benedict IX became the youngest head of the Roman Catholic Church, in 1032.

• 11: Beethoven turned professional.

• Seven: Chopin wrote his "Polonaise in G minor."

• Six: Shirley Temple won an Oscar.

• Three: John Stuart Mill was learning Greek. Elizabeth Taylor gave her first Royal Command Performance.

The Halifax explosion

On December 6, 1917, one-third of Halifax was destroyed when two ships collided in the harbour. They caused the largest man-made explosion in history, until the nuclear age:

• Fragments of the French munitions carrier *Mont Blanc* were blown 1.6 kilometres high when the ship's cargo – 2,766 tons of picric acid, TNT, and guncotton – was touched off at about 9 A.M.

• The blast, subsequent tidal wave, and raging fire destroyed 2.5 square kilometres of Halifax and blew apart a section of Dartmouth. Every pane of glass within 32 kilometres of the harbour was shattered; shock waves were felt 85 kilometres away. A 500-kilogram anchor shaft was pitched more than three kilometres across the city.

• Halifax had a population of less than 50,000 people: the blast killed 1,630 and injured 9,000 – including 200 blinded by flying glass. With 1,600 buildings destroyed and 12,000 damaged, there were 6,000 homeless and 20,000 people without adequate shelter.

• St. Paul's Anglican Church, three blocks from the harbour, survived the blast without structural damage.

• Robert Oppenheimer, the father of the atomic bomb, used the Halifax blast to predict the effect of his first device, according to a local geophysicist.

Names watch

• In 1803, Napoleon set up legislation to ban a name if it were "ridiculous" or "likely to provoke teasing." Judged illegal: Prune, Jade, Cerise, Manhattan, and Fleur de Marie.

• Sydney Biddle Barrows, in her book *Mayflower Madam*, says she picked a list of possible pseudonyms for her call girls by using baby-naming books. "Occasionally I would have to veto one of their suggestions, because names like Monique, Noelle, Nicole, and Tiffany made a girl sound like a hooker."

• Some English names of the past 130 years, noted by the *Daily Telegraph*: Rheumatism Rayment (born 1900); Windsor Castle (born 1876); Mineral Waters (born 1892); and Not Wanted James Colville (died 1861).

• Jane Fonda has two children, Vanessa and Troy – he is named after Nguyen Van Troi, who tried to kill the U.S. secretary of defence in 1966.

• At one time in Wales, largely because of a limited choice of surnames, it was not unusual, for instance, to have ten David Joneses in one village, according to the *Independent on Sunday*. This produced offbeat nicknames such as Evans Above (an undertaker), Dai Scab (his grandfather worked during a strike 70 years earlier), Amen Jones (a loud churchgoer), and Dai Bolical (a miner who never washed).

Pearl Harbor

December 7 is perhaps the most solemn date on the U.S. calendar. Some notes about the attack on Pearl Harbor in 1941:
• The attack's surprise and devastation were so complete that photographs of the event were nearly destroyed, on orders from old-line officers in the War Department. They feared bad public relations. It was two months before the public saw a heavily edited newsreel of the raid.
• The central memorial at Pearl is built over the half-sunk battleship *Arizona*, the tomb for 1,177 men. Visitors can see the main deck, three metres below the waves. There is still a rainbow slick on the water; every nine seconds a spurt of oil bleeds from the ship's innards and rises to the surface.
• The attack on Pearl Harbor – indeed, the entire four-year struggle – may have been scripted by a brilliant British naval correspondent. In 1926, Hector Bywater wrote *The Great Pacific War*, describing a U.S.-Japanese conflict that begins with a surprise attack on the U.S. navy and simultaneous

seizures of Guam and the Philippines. Admiral Isoroku Yamamoto, designer of the Pearl Harbor raid and a former military attache in Washington, met Mr. Bywater in 1934 and spent an entire evening discussing tactics. He adopted the Briton's ideas as his own.

Significant digits

• One: Dr. David Livingstone, the Victorian missionary in Africa, converted only one individual in 12 years – and that man, yearning for polygamy, later relapsed into paganism.

• Three: The world's population is growing by three people a second, says the *Daily Telegraph*, and a third of the globe's population is entering its reproductive years during the 1990s.

• Five to ten: A meteor is a shaft of light in the sky, often just a grain of dust. Every day there are several hundred million visible streakers, with many more too faint to be seen by the naked eye. On a average dark night, an observer will see five to ten an hour.

• Eight: Australia is creeping north-northeast at five to eight centimetres a year and could be one kilometre closer in as little as 20,000 years.

• 15: The odds that a person will have sex today are one in 15, writes Bob Berger in *Beating Murphy's Law*, a book obviously aimed at Americans.

• 20 to 60: "Private speech," or talking to oneself, can account for 20 to 60 per cent of the remarks made by a child younger than ten. (As much as that? Well, that's what the article in *Scientific American* said.)

• 30: "Those magnificent photographs of Earth . . . are the best photographs, and they were taken nearly 30 years ago," says Richard Underwood, who trained every U.S. astronaut who has ever used a camera in space. "The brilliant, clear, magnificent photos were the Gemini photos of the mid-1960s. The air pollution was a lot less then, and it shows."

• 64: "Something like 100 million people have come to Lourdes, France, in the past 136 years in the hope of being cured – many with diseases that modern medicine is, so far, helpless to defeat," writes Carl Sagan in *Parade* magazine. "The Roman Catholic Church has authenticated only 64 miraculous cures."

• 72: The normal life span of sperm is 72 hours.

• 74: Studies show that squirrels fail to recover about 74 per cent of the nuts they bury. This is good for reforestation.

• 75: A baby is 75 per cent water by weight, compared with 60 to 65 per cent for an adult man.

Ipanema goodbye

On December 9, 1994, 67-year-old composer Antonio Carlos Jobim was buried in Rio de Janeiro. He was Brazil's best-loved composer and probably the most famous, writes Kerry Luft of the *Chicago Tribune*. In a bar in 1963, Mr. Jobim and a poet friend turned out "The Girl from Ipanema" – about a beautiful teenager they used to see walking to the beach. (The men were too shy to talk to her or to identify her, until the song became a hit.) The song has since been recorded 180 times and translated into several languages, including Japanese. In 1994, Helo Pinheiro – 47, but still tall and tanned, and lovely – threw a long-stemmed rose on Mr. Jobim's coffin as it passed by, and turned away. The crowd, which hadn't noticed her at first, began singing.

The telephone

This holiday season, people can phone their relatives or their loved ones. Some notes about the phone:

• Alexander Graham Bell said the idea for the telephone came to him in Brantford, Ontario, in the summer of 1874.

• Bell's granddaughter recalled in 1950: "Grandfather never said 'Hello' on the telephone, and it exasperated him that this greeting had become general, instead of 'Hoy, hoy,' which he considered more euphonious."

• In 1877, Massachusetts businessman Charles Williams installed the first private line – in his home, so his wife could reach him during the day.

• In 1878, Emma M. Nutt became the first female telephone operator. Previously, young boys had been used but their language proved to be unsuitable.

• In 1879, exchanges listed only the names of subscribers, who resented numbers as an affront to their individuality.

• In 1889, William Gray invented the pay phone after he had been refused a call to his sick wife from work.

• In 1915, to inaugurate transcontinental service, Bell repeated his "Mr. Watson, come here" message. This time his assistant, Thomas A. Watson, was in San Francisco and he replied it would take him a week. (Sources: *The Canadian Inventions Book*, *Baltimore Sun*, wire services.)

Pole's notes

The South Pole was reached on December 14, 1911, by Roald Amundsen. Because of a navigation error, his British rival, Robert Scott, missed the pole by one kilometre the following month. Except for an overflight in 1929, no one visited the pole again until 1956. In the winter, it is sometimes colder at the South Pole than it is on the surface of Mars. The world's lowest temperature was recorded at Vostok, Antarctica, in 1983: minus 89.2 degrees Celsius.

Old fallguy

On December 14, 1417, Sir John Oldcastle was executed in England. Descendants of the Catholic heretic objected to William Shakespeare using the knight's name for a fat, buffoonish character. Under pressure, Shakespeare changed the name to Falstaff and denied any connection with Sir John.

In the swim

This holiday season, some Canadians will travel to climates where swimming is pleasant. A sprinkling of notes about the aquatic pastime:
• Swimming was practised about 2500 BC in Egypt and later in Assyria, Greece, and Rome.
• In the Middle Ages, Europeans scorned swimming. The lack of outdoor bathing is explained by some authorities as a fear the practice was unhealthy. Also, religious fables equated swimmers with the "ungodly." Not until the 19th century did swimming again become as popular as it had been during classical times – and the English were acknowledged as the best swimmers in the world, writes Charles Sprawson in *Haunts of the Black Masseur: The Swimmer As Hero*.
• Swimming was first regarded as a quirky, aristocratic pastime that appealed to the Romantics and lovers of classical times. Lord Byron swam the dangerous Hellespont and often boasted about it. (One night after a party in Venice, he jumped fully

clothed into the Grand Canal and swam back to his digs, holding a blazing torch aloft to avoid the gondola traffic.) Percy Shelley was very keen on water, although he couldn't swim. (He drowned while boating in a storm.) As a lad, the poet Matthew Arnold worried his father by spending an entire summer holiday imagining himself to be a corpse at the bottom of Lake Windermere.

Seasonal gathering

• A 40-year-old Edinburgh woman called Anne is a well-known shoplifter, reported the *Independent* in 1993. That Yuletide season, department stores were displaying a warning picture of the woman, who was well-known to her neighbours. "People are always coming up and saying, 'The money's on the table if you can get me this for the children.' This is the busiest time of the year for me," said Anne. "It's been crazy. I have not had time to do my own Christmas shoplifting yet."
• People purchasing firewood should knock several pieces together. Unseasoned wood will produce a dull thud, but seasoned timber will crack like a bat hitting a baseball.

Christmas cards

Modern versions of Christmas cards can be very specialized. A recent U.S. Christmas card for ailing former spouses said, "Sorry to hear you're not feeling well. I wouldn't want anything to stop the alimony payments." Some Christmas-card greetings on sale in Toronto in 1990:
• "To a Fine News Carrier."
• "For you, doctor, at Christmas."
• "From Our Dog Especially for You."

Unchanging Christmas

Christmas is losing its real meaning, agreed 59 per cent of
Canadians – back in 1953. (The Canadian Institute of Public
Opinion reported that this was a 6-per-cent jump from its
survey of 1948.) Some not-so-different Christmas news in
Globe files of a generation ago:

• 1953. Canadian author Farley Mowat said in an interview,
"As for that song 'Dreaming of a White Christmas' – I loathe
it! If I hear it once more, I'm going to toss my radio into the
ashcan."

• 1954. New York City police arrested one of Santa's helpers
near Times Square because he was snarling "You cheap son of
a bitch" at anyone who ignored his collection box.

• December 24, 1955. Mary Marcos of Nazareth, on a trip to
Bethlehem to celebrate Christmas Eve, gave birth to a son.
Jordanians informed the Israeli authorities and found room
for Ms. Marcos to remain on the Arab side of the armistice
line for another week.

• December 24, 1956. Two black men were finally served at a
restaurant in Dresden, Ontario. The owner had given up his
battle for the right to refuse service to negroes. Dresden is
notable as the place where the original Uncle Tom is buried.

• December 23, 1957. Maria Golinksa of Warsaw spent seven
hours – and half her family's monthly income – buying food,
drink, and a Christmas tree. "After all," she told a Western
journalist, "life is hard enough the rest of the year."

• 1958. Three Christian ministers in Ontario said that Christ
should be taken out of Christmas, because the holiday has its
roots in pagan festivals that did not involve Him. "It seems
sort of religious imperialism," said Rev. J. Franklin Chidsey, a

Unitarian. "If we celebrated Christmas as a happy holiday instead of a Christian feast, people of every religion would be able to enjoy it together."

Hogtown Christmas

In 1839, Toronto printer William Lyon Mackenzie docked his office boy 66 cents for being absent Christmas and New Year's Day, reports the Toronto Historical Board.

Dee-dee-dee-dah . . .

Consider if you will Rodman Serling (1925-75), a writer in a hurry. He was born on December 25. Jewish – but not religious about it. He was a teller of parables, a believer in traditional virtues, and a wordsmith with a purple streak. Diminutive, but a giant in the Golden Age of television, Mr. Serling achieved lasting fame unexpectedly in . . . "The Twilight Zone":

• The television series is more autobiographical than many viewers realize, writes biographer Gordon Sander. Episodes were sometimes based on his nightmares and stories he had been reading (a sore point with a few other writers). Also, the extroverted Mr. Serling grew up in "hidebound, anti-Semitic" Binghamton, New York. This was the pastoral, small, "Twilight Zone" town to which he returned, literally and imaginatively, for the rest of his life, and he wasn't blind to its failings.

• In the Second World War, Mr. Serling brazened his way past the height requirements and became a paratrooper. His unit fought the Japanese day and night in the jungles of the Philippines. He rarely talked about the war afterward and, although patriotic, became an early anti-nuclear activist and opponent of the U.S. presence in Vietnam.

• After the war, Mr. Serling enrolled at Antioch, a liberal college in Ohio where women "openly smoked cigarettes and wore pants." He met his wife and continued the writing he had begun in the war as therapy. Much of it was junk, but he was learning to write adequately for the infant medium of television. (To support his family, he also tested parachutes occasionally for the U.S. army, at $25 a jump.) Early on, Carol Serling corrected his spelling and eventually came to rule this "man-child" who admitted he could never write women's roles convincingly.

• Mr. Serling was prolific, perhaps the most productive writer in TV history. He wrote three award-winning teleplays – *Patterns, The Comedians*, and *Requiem for a Heavyweight* – which are considered U.S. television classics. Hungry for approval, he also accepted every assignment he was offered and wrote too much. However, this meant he had a rejected time-travel fantasy script available that was the seed for "The Twilight Zone."

• Journalists referred to Mr. Serling as an angry young man. Censorship rankled him. For instance, despising prejudice, he tried twice to dramatize the lynching in the mid-fifties of a 14-year-old black youngster in Mississippi. For the first production, the sponsor demanded that the story be set in New England, that the word "lynch" be dropped, that bottles of Coca-Cola be removed, and that the characters speak grammatically and make comments such as, "This is a strange little town." The second time, the sponsor was an insurance company and the sheriff in Mr. Serling's story couldn't kill himself because suicide often led to problems in the claims department.

- "To public and press alike," writes author Marc Zicree, "Serling was viewed as video's equivalent of Arthur Miller or Tennessee Williams." In 1959, hearing he was going to write and produce a science-fiction series, TV newsman Mike Wallace asked Mr. Serling, "(So) you've given up writing anything important for television, right?"

- During 1959-64, Mr. Serling used "The Twilight Zone" (the name comes from a term that airline pilots use when they descend so close to the runway that the horizon disappears and they feel abruptly imbalanced) to write offbeat fables, sometimes with downbeat endings and social criticisms that would otherwise have been commercially unacceptable. Although never a big hit in that period, the show grew more popular in reruns and is one of a handful of series that are continually in circulation.

- In five years, Mr. Serling wrote 90 of the 156 episodes. His last years were spent teaching, shilling products on television, and quixotically attempting to write teleplays such as a nonviolent Western series.

- A nervous, compulsive man, Mr. Serling smoked so much that his doctor advised him to cut back to one pack a day. In the summer of 1975 he had three heart attacks – the last, which killed him, occurred during open-heart surgery. (Sources: *Globe* files, *The Twilight Zone Companion, Rod Serling: The Dreams and Nightmares of Life in The Twilight Zone, Serling: The Rise and Twilight of Television's Last Angry Man*.

Le jour D'iddley

December 30 is the birthday of Bo Diddley, born in 1928. The vintage rocker – he was born Ellas McDaniel and acquired his nickname while attending grade school in Chicago – is the originator of the distinctive "Bo Diddley beat," for which he has received scant money or recognition. Here's some leftover news items that may amount to diddly:

• In the next century, humans will return to the moon. One of the big attractions, according to the *Journal of the British Interplanetary Society*, is tourism – and lovemaking in lunar hotels. Not only will a greater variety of sexual positions be possible, "the very act of making love on the moon will last much longer than it does here, because people's bodies will move so much more slowly," said Dr. Andrew Stanway, a British sex expert. "And every lover will automatically be six times lighter." The only drawback he can foresee is gliding down from the roof and missing the bed.

• Although breast tumours are equally likely to occur on either side of the body, left-breast tumours are detected earlier, according to Minneapolis surgeon Leonard Schultz. He attributes this to the fact that most husbands are right-handed.

• The dominance of right-handed people has been attributed, by one academic theory of recent years, to a seabed-dwelling, Jurassic ancestor of humans that had a rudimentary left ear in its anus. This caused the creature to lie permanently on its side, writes Alan Hamilton in the *Times* of London, and grab passing prey with its right paw.

• Typewriters were not widely accepted until 1909; few people wanted to pay $125 (U.S.) to replace pens with nibs that cost a penny. Companies then hired women demonstrators, called "typewriters," to visit offices; purchasers often said they would buy the machines if they were accompanied by the women. Typewriters are credited for the subsequent influx of women into the business world.

New Year's Eve

To prevent a hangover: uncork wine to let it breathe –
the hangover-causing "congeners" evaporate faster
than the alcohol; take food or drink high in fruc-
tose (including tomato juice, honey, apples, and
grapes), which increases the rate at which the
body breaks down alcohol; line the stomach with high-
protein food; use cold compresses, caffeine, and ASA to reduce
the swelling of the brain vessels; don't drink too much; don't
drink at all.

The tabloids say . . .

• Worker killed tying his shoe: he and pal bend over at the
same time and conk heads (*Weekly World News*).
• Judge lets drug suspect go free – cops didn't count to 15
before arresting him (*National Enquirer*).
• Cat's breath kills man (*Sun*).
• Missing $15 million found year later – in the closet (*National
Examiner*).
• "All of a sudden I was attacked from inside by a kicking baby."
(*National Enquirer*).

Thought du month

"The man who doesn't read good books has no advantage over
the man who can't read them." – Mark Twain.